Dark Psychology

Enter The World Of Dark Psychology And
Discover Secret Manipulation Techniques
Ranging From The Subtle Art Of Getting
What You Want To Weapons of Emotional
Mass Destruction

I0540758

Robert D. Sykes

Dark Psychology:

Enter The World Of Dark Psychology And Discover Secret Manipulation Techniques Ranging From The Subtle Art Of Getting What You Want To Weapons of Emotional Mass Destruction

Copyright © 2019 by Robert D. Sykes

Table Of Contents:

Introduction

You wake up at four in the morning on your day off. You're panting, sweating, and are inexplicably anxious. You can't remember having a dream. You can't recall eating or drinking anything before going to bed to induce such a horrible waking experience.

So, what's wrong with you?

Perhaps it's something much darker than you realize. Perhaps someone has targeted you and you've been completely unaware of it.

Does someone want what you have?

As humans, we've learned to accumulate certain things and people to make our lives as easy as possible. We find a mate to share our lives with and the responsibilities that come along with our lives. We find a job to pay for all the things we're going to not only need but want. We buy a home to raise our family in. We buy the things we need, like automobiles to transport our families and us to where we need to go.

So far, we've got a pretty good list of things people feel that they need: a mate – a job – a home – a car. And we're willing to work for these things. But not everyone is willing to work the way we are.

Some people wish to take the lazy way in life. They would rather let someone else accumulate these things, then they will edge in, push you out of the way and take over everything you worked so hard for.

Don't fool yourself into thinking this idea is far-fetched and not worth worrying about. Think about how many divorces there are. Think about how many times you've found someone eyeing your mate, your job, your home, your car. Now, think about the stories you've heard of people going missing. Someone has to take over what they left behind, right?

Someone has to come into the distraught mate's life who was left all alone. Someone has to take over the job they left vacant. Someone has to move into the home to take the place left by the vacant mate. And someone has to drive the car they left too. Many believe that it might as well be them. And some would prefer not to wait for someone to pass on from natural causes before they take over what will be left behind.

Insidious, you say?

I agree it is. And it happens all the time.

Not everyone will kill to replace someone. Many merely use mental techniques to acquire what they desire. They learn how to get into other people's heads to make them do what they want them to.

They can get into your head, the head of your boss, and even the head of your mate. They can warp things to bend in their favor while making you seem inadequate in ways you had no idea you were. They might even make you feel as if you should let them have what you've worked for − as if they're better equipped to deal with things than you are.

Even the most secure individuals can be made to feel insecure. They can be made to feel as if they're not entirely sane and not seeing things the right way. Once you think that maybe you're wrong about something, you've already given someone else the upper hand.

Not that you should always think you're right about every little thing. No one is right about everything. But beware of that person who is telling you that you are not what you think you are. Beware of the person who doles out backhanded compliments to you. Beware of that person who tells you often how *lucky* you are to have what you do.

Luck has nothing to do with what you've gotten for yourself and your life. Hard work, perseverance, and using your brain has gotten you where you are today. Luck had little to nothing to do with it.

In this book, I'll let you in on some secrets that you can keep a lookout for. There's no reason for you to wake up in a panicked state again. If some dark individual comes snooping around you and what you've made of your life, you will recognize them quickly and get rid of them. You will defend that life you built against anyone who threatens it. And you will do so, using the same techniques the darkness wanted to use against you.

It's time to learn how to get into the minds of what some consider monsters. I hope you're ready.

Chapter 1: Enter the Dark Side

Chapter 1.1: A Well-Kept Secret

Dark psychology, what's it all about?

Let's start with the definition of psychology. It is the study of the human mind and behavior.

If knowledge is power, then having vast knowledge of normal psychology is comparable to having super-powers. And who among us doesn't want to have super-powers?

Psychology is used in almost every aspect of our daily lives. When we turn on our televisions – if you have commercial television of course – we will find marketing gurus using psychology to make us believe we *need* the products they're selling.

The things being sold nowadays covers things marketing never had to cover in the past. You can even find commercials that pertain to religions. The marketing geniuses use the power of psychology to get us to go to the church they've been paid to get us to attend.

Why is that?

To make money of course. Even churches make money off the people who attend their services. Does that make them evil?

Does it make you evil to take money for the work you do?

What about love?

There are so many dating apps out in the world today that if you're lonely, you just haven't looked hard enough. Farmers, ranchers, scientists, nerds, dorks, and even people with the oddest fetishes on record can find love if they merely search for the right website or app. And that is all thanks to people who have found that using psychology can be profitable.

People who understand psychological principles have the keys to influencing others. Although learning all the ins and outs of psychology isn't easy, it can be done without spending tons of money on taking college courses.

In the past, one had to go to many years of college to gain even a remote understanding of human psychology. And even then, they may have been left not clearly understanding everything they were taught or read in ancient journals and texts.

Mountains of books had to be gone through. Countless lectures had to be sat through as professors droned on about Socrates, Plato, and Aristotle. Ancient philosophers were at the forefront of the science that morphed into present-day psychology.

The human mind is a complex thing. As such, many people have sought to understand what makes people tick, do the things they do, and act the way they act. Tons of material had to be gone through and lots of it had to be sifted out of what would become thought of as true and proven psychological insight.

In the midst of all this enlightenment, there came a term used to describe heinous acts – dark psychology. Dark psychology is very real and very much a threat to us all. It is in every part of this world we live in. It is very much a part of every day that you wake up and start interacting in any way with others. Even if you only turn on your television or radio.

There's nothing you can do to change or stop dark psychology from happening. But you can do something about the way you react to it when it's used on you. And you can train your brain to spot it.

As always, with anything - you do have choices. You can refuse to believe that something as sinister sounding as dark psychology exists. After all, there is good and evil, and they are as black and white and obvious as night and day. Who needs to try to learn about some mysterious nothing that's being touted so often nowadays? Not you?

Are you sure about that?

Being ruthless isn't such a taboo thing to be in this day and age. To pull one over on someone – especially, to make a buck – is thought to be clever. And most people think that everyone does it anyway, so why shouldn't they?

Think about the selling of cigarettes that started so long ago that most younger people have no idea how long these things have even been around.

Doctors suggested smoking to pregnant mothers, to help calm their nerves. A cigarette along with a glass of beer, wine, or other spirits would do wonders for the pregnant mother and her developing baby. At least that was the popular opinion of physicians in the forties, fifties, sixties, and even into the early seventies.

The marketers went for every personality they could think of too. They marketed to the rich. They used movie stars to help build the market too. Smoking was prevalent in movies and on television in an era that wouldn't allow television shows to show a married couple's bedroom unless there were two – separate beds in it. And if there was a kiss in the scene, at least one foot had to remain on the floor. Yet, the cancer sticks they smoked were not only in the acts, they sometimes were huge parts of the acts.

Are you starting to see how sinister things can be now?

I want you to think about any movie or television show in which someone has a laptop computer. Now, you know that there are many different companies that make laptop computers. But you will never find someone opening a Dell computer in any movie. You won't find them opening an HP laptop. Even the desktop computers you see in the movies and on television share one common trait. They are all Apple computers.

Let's be real here. Apple computers are not the top-selling brand of computers. So, why are they so prevalent in films?

You guessed it – money.

Dark psychology is at work in the world, whether you choose to believe it or not. You might not like this fact, but you can't change it. So you have a choice. Either remain ignorant of something so powerful that it can make you put poison into your body without giving it a second thought. You can take the risk of becoming the next victim of the darkness.

But you don't have to do that at all. You can take control of your situation. You can learn to protect yourself. You can learn to protect the people you love from people who wish to ruin others through pitiless psychological abuse.

Let us take a look at the various places where we can find dark psychology being used, shall we?

Politics is the first thing that comes to my mind – probably yours too.

Politicians seem to be set on getting themselves into office, no matter what the heck they have to say to get themselves there. And why is that, do you suppose?

Power. Plain and simple, it is to gain power over others.

Sure, some seek office to help others. We all know there are a handful of truthful politicians out there in the world. But there is a heck of a lot more immoral, dark-minded – power-hungry people out there who want to be paid to control those they are supposed to serve.

You can simply open your computer, turn on your radio, or your television to hear politicians telling you how you need to think. They want to tell you how to vote, who to vote for, where to vote, and what at what time you should do it.

Becoming the governor of a state gives a person more power than most people realize. They don't have to go through the senate and congress to pass laws they deem worthy. There's still red tape they must wade through but it's nothing compared to what the President of the United States has to deal with. Furthermore, people who've sat in the governor's chair are more likely to be backed by others to run for the presidential office. Talk about some power!

And we've all seen what people will do to get into the White House. Why would so many politicians want to get into the White House when every president in history had to deal with naysayers and ridicule? Everlasting power is why that is.

Once you serve as president, you've got the ear and attention of the entire world. Who wouldn't want that kind of recognition and status?

Not to say any names because no one wants to get on their bad side, but there's an ex-presidential family right now who seems to have tremendous influence and power that doesn't quite make sense. Although scandal became woven into the fabric of the eight-year presidency, still many people are willing to do the bidding of this family.

One can only imagine what dark forces lie behind political figures. When people are willing to not only lie, but also cheat, and steal to gain what they want, others must be wary of those types of people.

So, let's look at the next place one might run into people who are actively practicing dark psychology. The workplace can be a cut-throat world for many people.

The job can be anything at all and still you will find people willing to cut others out so they can have more. From waitresses who will race to gain a table full of high paying customers to the management of your local grocery store, you will find people who seek to step on others to make themselves look better than the rest.

You may have been the victim of someone who used you to gain a reputation for great work when they didn't do a thing except rely on you to make them look good. They made more money than you and received recognition for the work you did.

Fair?

No way.

But the thing is that you didn't have to play into their hands in the first place. There are some valid reasons to go above your boss's head after all. If you feel as if you're being exploited and perhaps have been told that your job is on the line if you don't do as they want you to, then you do have a resource available to you. The Human Resources department can be your best friend when it comes to bosses or even just co-workers who are trying to use or belittle you.

None of us *have* to become victims. We all have the same rights as anyone trying to victimize you have. We have the right to say, no. And we have the right not to give a reason for our answer. We have the right to walk away. And we have the right not to explain why we're doing it.

The thing with people who thrive on using dark psychology to get what they want is that they need a person to stand there, listen to what they have to say and to act on what they want you to act on. It's all up to you if you actually do it or not.

The longer you listen to a person who is trying to use you to get what they want, the easier it is for them to say the right words that will hit your brain in a way that you never imagined could happen to you.

Let's move on and go to the one place everyone feels safe – religions. In most cases, the words being said by the people in charge – the ministers, preachers, pastors, and priests – are meant to lift their congregations. But there are some who only want to get others to do what they want while getting them to give them everything they have.

Many cult leaders use the power of dark psychology to get their followers to do as they tell them to. They use scare tactics most of the time. End of the world kind of stuff is used to frighten people into not only believing everything their leaders say, but they will also move into compounds with their leaders and other followers and they will bring along every last thing they've ever accumulated in life to give to the compound and their leader.

Many of these cults have ended in tragedy. I find it kind of ironic that their leaders prophesized bad things for their followers. But it wasn't the world that put the people in danger, it was the people they followed who did that.

It's important to live this life, learning as you go. But you must never allow anyone to tell you things and you merely accept them as facts. You have to do your own research and you have to come up with what you believe, instead of blindly following others.

Another place we think we're safe is within our various relationships — not only romantic ones but ones within your family and friends as well. When we're children, we don't have any choice in who our parents are or following their rules. But as we all know, once children get old` enough to start exercising their own judgment, that's when they begin to argue with their parents even if the rule has always been in place. "That's not fair," is a term echoed around most homes each and every day.

People can have rules for their family and their home. But what if the rules or practices that are going on within a home and family are detrimental to the people in it?

This happens a lot and we can see it on the news almost every day.

One of the cases that come to mind of some terrible abuse of power is the case of a child being kept in a cage meant to house an animal. And what was this child to do in order for the poor thing not to be locked in a cage?

Here's the thing, not only children are done this way. Some adults have been locked away in cages and other places. Why is it that they came to a place in their minds that made them go along with being locked up?

In some cases, there was the use of force, maybe a gun or knife had them feeling it was a threat against their lives and they felt the safer route was just to do as they were told to. In other cases, the victim somewhat willingly went into the cage.

Here is where you can plainly see that dark psychology was used to get the person to do as the enforcer wanted. And the thing is that all things that people who use dark psychology don't always gain them anything more than the knowledge that they had the power to do what they did.

Some people who seek to steer others into a direction they desire, don't do it for money, or things. Some people only do it to prove to themselves that they can.

That's a little frightening, I know. So, it's important for you to learn how to spot when someone is trying to do this to you or someone you love. It's important to learn all you can about the darkness. Not so you can use it to get what you want. But so you can use it to stop others and yourself from falling victim to it.

Chapter 1.2: Never Trust The Smiley Guy

People with lots of charisma can be extremely influencing. There is a reason that salespeople always dress their very best and keep their appearance immaculate. They're trying to project to others that they have it all together. And since they do, you should want to do as they say to.

Don't you want to be the type of person who has it all together?

These people never come at you with a frown and a finger-wagging in your face, telling you what you have to do. They came at you, armed with a smile that is meant to make you focus on them and how awesome they are and how you would be so smart and awesome too if you did what they told you to do.

Beware of those who come at you with smiles on their faces for no apparent reason. They are seeking to gain something from you. It's not often the case that they have something they want to give you without any strings attached what-so-ever.

Chapter 1.3: Falling For Deception

Unfortunately for us humans, we're hardwired to accept people at face value. We're brought up by parents who don't always tell us the truth. Think about Santa and the Easter Bunny for starters.

Evolution is to blame for the way we begin our lives. It was important for a parent to keep their children alive. Populating the planet was job number one at the beginning of time.

Children are curious by nature, making it hard for parents to stop their kids from wandering into the lions' den. So, they came up with scary tales to get their kids to stop wandering off and to stick close to home where it was safe.

Everything plays a role in why we believe things that simply aren't true. Genetics, history, even the education we receive forms our minds in ways that make some of us more vulnerable to becoming victims of users of dark psychology.

The news isn't all bad though. Being hardwired the way we all are means that we can build entire societies and the structures that make life easier for all of us.

But there are people with darker sides. The Dark Triad is made up of three personality disorders that you need to know about. Narcissism, Machiavellianism, and psychopathy are the three things you have to look out for. These people are more than just hardwired the way most of us are. These people have serious mental issues that make them unable to feel human emotions the way people without these disorders do. They hurt others just to do it and feel no remorse or guilt for doing it.

Neurolinguistic Programming or NLP is a way to develop techniques to influence people. This is a subject worth going deeper into really understanding the kind of human nature nobody wants to openly share. I encourage you to check out my other book on this topic:

Dark Psychology: Discover The Trade's Secret NLP Techniques And Cheat Codes Using Covert Manipulation, Mind Control, Hypnosis And Other Forbidden Techniques —With Practical Exercises And Case Studies

I would like for you to feel free to give me your input and insights into the subject of NLP and dark psychology in general. You can join my inner circle board or contact me directly at analyis221b@gmail.com

Key Takeaways

1. Dark psychology is the study of the human mind and why we do devious, unconscionable acts, with evil intent.

2. Dark psychology is used in religion, politics, relationships, in advertisements, and at work.

3. The Dark Triad is made up of three distinct personality disorders - Narcissism, Machiavellianism, and psychopathy.

4. NLP is neurolinguistic programming and it's used in all sorts of things nowadays, from dating apps to modern psychological therapies.

5. You can join my inner circle board here analyis221b@gmail.com

Exercises

If you see a man begging on the street and you've seen him around before, driving a nice car, working at a respectable job, and living in a nice home what would you do?

If someone you care about comes to you with a story about someone bullying them, what would you tell them?

You are at work and your boss comes to you, asking to see the presentation you've come up with and he ends up taking it with him, telling you to write another that this one just won't work. Later, you are at the presentation meeting and he uses the presentation you wrote, and he took and calls it his own. What are you going to do about that?

Some people believe that when life hands you lemons, you make lemonade. Others just look like they take the lemons and suck on them, leaving them with sour faces and puckered lips. Which type are you and why?

Chapter 2: How To Master The Puppet Show

Chapter 2.1: Introduction

What are covert manipulation and emotional exploitation?

And why do you need to know about this?

When you are unaware of things, you can fall victim to them. If you don't know what to look for, then you can be hurt by what finds you.

Covert is an easy term to understand. It means that it's an act of secrecy and is hidden from plain sight. Think about a spy and you will begin to visualize the meaning of covert.

Emotional exploitation refers to using one's emotions against them such as drawing out fear in a person or sadness in them and then using those emotions to get them to see things your way or gain something from them. In laymen's terms, you use whatever you can to make a person feel - sad, afraid, excited, happy, or any other emotion you can think of and maybe even combinations of emotions, to alter their perception of things so you can get out of them what you want.

So, let's get to some typical mental manipulations then.

If someone tries to make you feel guilty about everything, they're using your emotion of guilt to get to you. What's the point in that, you ask?

Simply to prove to themselves that they can make you feel any way they want to.

Take this example:

Mary made John a nice dinner. She thought she'd made some of his favorites. But once the meal was done, she asked, "Did you like it?"

John shrugs. "Well, it was okay. I mean, I wanted something else. But you liked it and you made it, so all that really matters is that you enjoyed it."

"But I made it with you in mind." She frowns with disappointment.

"Oh, no." He smiles and pats her on the back. "Don't look like that. I want you to be happy. I really do. If that means having a meal that you think you made with me in mind, when you really were thinking about what you would like, that's fine with me. I love you, honey. Whatever makes you happy makes me happy."

You can see how he influenced her into feeling guilty and even put the idea in her head that she subconsciously thought about herself over him. Pretty eerie, isn't it?

Some people will put their insecurities on you. This happens a lot in romantic relationships. They hold you accountable for things that happened to them in the past and have nothing to do with your moral character.

Lacy and Joe have been dating for months. Lacy wants to have a girl's night out but Joe isn't feeling secure about that. "You know that Bonnie would go out with her friends and cheat on me, right?"

"Yeah, but I'm not Bonnie. *I* am Lacy and *I* do not cheat, Joe. So, you have nothing to worry about." She keeps getting dressed to meet her friends for a few drinks.

Joe sighs and sits on the end of the bed, looking gloomy. "Yeah, but I'm not feeling happy with this. It would make me happy if you just didn't do that sort of thing. We can have a few drinks together. You know – just me and you. I'll make it fun. I promise."

Lacy turns her attention to him. "Joe, I love hanging out with you and you know that. I adore you, babe. But I need a little girl-time. I haven't hung out with my friends since we started dating over six months ago. They miss me."

"And you don't care that I'll be worried the entire time until you get back home?" He looks like he's about to puke and holds his stomach.

Lacy can't help but feel for the man she loves. "Joe, I love you. Can't you just trust me? I mean, I trusted you to go out after work with your co-workers. Can't you trust me to do the same thing?"

"I wasn't the cheater, Lacy. I know I'm trustworthy."

What is Lacy to do?

Along with projecting their own insecurities on you, they can twist things you've done to make you feel as if you don't truly know yourself.

Lacy doesn't want to give into Joe. "I know that I am also trustworthy, Joe."

"I didn't want to bring this up, but I think you should hear something about yourself that you might not even realize that you do." He sighs, acting as if he doesn't want to bring up the subject at all, but she's forcing him to. "You flirt, Lacy. I don't think you mean to, but you do it all the time. When we're checking out at the grocery store, you flirt with the bag boys. And that time we went to the movies and you wanted popcorn. You batted your eyelashes at the guy who got it for you and asked him if he could possibly give you some extra butter – on the house."

"I did not bat my eyelashes at that kid." Lacy is left trying to think back to if she'd really done such a thing. "I don't mean to flirt. I don't think I really do that at all."

"Well, you do. I can see it. Any man can see it. And that's what scares me is that you'll flirt, and some man will take it the wrong way and the next thing I know, you're dancing with some random dude and I'm sitting home eating leftover chicken pot pie."

"You're being silly." Lacy doesn't want to give in, even though Joe has already played on her emotions and her own insecurities.

Now he's on to the next trick. He's angry that she's not listening to him and doing as he wants her to.

"Don't call me names!" He gets up and walks out of the room, slamming the door behind him.

Lacy never meant to make him angry and it bothers her. She gets up to go after him. "Joe! Come on, babe. Don't be mad."

"That must've been what you wanted me to feel. You should think about why you would want to make a man you claim to love, feel angry. What does that say about you, Lacy?"

She looks thoroughly confused. "I – well, I didn't mean to make you mad, Joe."

Now he has to make her believe that she wants what he does.

"Don't you want to have a happy relationship, Lacy? I mean, I thought you and I were on the same page here. I thought we both wanted to be in a relationship where we strove to make the other person happy. I had no idea we were in a one-sided deal where you get to do whatever you want, and I just deal with it. I guess I was wrong. I guess we aren't on the same page."

"No," she says as she takes his hand. "Don't feel like that. I do want to make you happy. I just wanted to make my friends happy too. They've been after me for a long time to meet up with them for a few drinks and to talk about how our lives are going. I really wanted to tell them how happy I've been with you."

"So, that's more important to you than making me happy by not going in the first place?"

You can see here how hard this is for Lacy. She's not sure what to do. She doesn't want to fight. She doesn't want her man to feel he's not worth her trying to make happy.

Some people are easier to emotionally abuse than others. And the thing is that people who seek to rule over another person, don't deal with people who refuse to be emotionally whipped. They just move on to the next person until they find what they need.

For instance, if Lacy would've told Joe that she was going out with her friends and that it is completely acceptable to do so, he would see her as a person he couldn't manipulate emotionally.

What would Joe do when Lacy repeatedly refuses to let him control her emotions? What would Joe do when Lacy refused to deviate her plans to make him happy?

You know what he would do. He would end that relationship because she wasn't going to meet his needs. And she would be better off for it too.

But some people - people who are easier to manipulate - won't see what he's doing at all. They will see shortcomings in themselves instead.

Things don't have to be this way. You can effectively stop people in your life right now who are doing this to you.

So let's not talk about they why's and how're the manipulators have. Let's talk about you and what you can do.

First, you should try to understand why you allow yourself to be manipulated in the first place. You can go back to your childhood for this answer. Perhaps you were ignored by your parents. Maybe your parents weren't big on adoration and you missed out on that.

You will seek these basic needs, to be listened to and loved by others if your parents neglected to give these things to you. And let's face it, not everyone is cut out to be the perfect parent. As a matter of fact, there can't be a perfect parent or a perfect anything for that matter so don't beat yourself or your parents up over the past. Instead, understand this about yourself and refuse to go to anyone to look for these things.

Find it within yourself. Love yourself. Listen to yourself.

If you can find the basic needs everyone has – to be loved, to be listened to, to be allowed to live a normal social life – within yourself, you've won the internal battle with yourself and no one else can use you to feed their inflated egos.

Beware of things that make you feel all bubbly inside. For instance, flattery is a thing you have to be wary of especially if you haven't done a thing to deserve it.

If someone tells you how pretty you are and you've worked to look that way, then say thank you. If you rolled out of bed, went to the store in a wrinkled t-shirt and sweatpants, and someone tells you that you're pretty, then they're falsely flattering you and have an agenda.

Being aware of what others are doing, or attempting to do to you, is the biggest key to not becoming a victim.

Chapter 2.2: Positive Reinforcement

Most of us have been in a situation where we relied on someone else to tell us if we look okay or not. Say, you're on the beach – no mirrors around at all. You get splashed in the face by a huge wave and feel like your mascara might have run.

"Hey, Jill, is my face looking okay?"

She barely glances at you. "Sure."

You don't feel as if she's taken a proper look at you and run your hands over your face then looking at them and you find some black trails in your hands. "Jill, come on. Look at me and tell me if I've got black stuff on my face. I don't want to look like an idiot out here."

Looking right at you, she gives you a smile. "You're absolutely fine. I think you might've had some mascara smear, but you've seemed to have wiped it off. Now stop worrying about what you look like and just have fun, Mandy. Geeze. This day isn't about being a glamour queen. It's about having some fun in the sun."

Although Mandy knows the day is about having fun, she doesn't want to look like a drunken raccoon. So, she shuts up and when the day ends, she goes to the car. And there she finds her face has black smudges all over it.

As embarrassment overcomes her, she hears Jill flirting it up with some guys they met earlier. And she's making a date while Mandy tries not to cry.

This isn't the first time her friend has let her look like a fool just so she can look better and get more attention.

Chapter 2.3: Negative Reinforcement

While we all know people who will tell you that you look good when you don't. We all know someone who will tell you that you look bad when you don't.

Getting someone to feel inadequate is a thing that people who like to pull other people's strings love to do. After all, if you can make someone who looks great, feel ugly, then you're quite the masterful manipulator.

Joe has on a brand new pair of shoes, some awesomely fitting jeans and has a fresh haircut for his date with the girl he's been after forever. His roommate hasn't always been that supportive of a guy, so he's not even going to ask him what he thinks about his appearance.

But as he's about to leave for his date, Jake stops him with one comment, "You wearing that shirt, man?"

"Uh, yeah. Why?" Joe asks, even though he doesn't care what Jake thinks at all and knows he's just a jerk who likes to get into people's heads.

Jake shrugs. "I don't know. It's green and you've got blue eyes. It just doesn't do much for you is what I'm saying. And Jill is the girl of your dreams. Plus, she's got lots of guys who are after her. You ought to think about that before you go out on a date with her, looking drab is all I'm saying."

Joe looks in the mirror near the front door. "I don't feel drab."

"But a black or blue shirt would perk your look up is all I'm saying. Plus, those shoes look like they're too big for you. Are you going for the appearance of big feet when you don't have them or what? I mean, I'm just curious. I have no idea what your game is, Joe."

Joe looks at his feet. "They look fine to me. I just bought these. They fit like a glove."

"Oh, really?" Jake puts his magazine down and gives Joe the once over. "Sure, I guess you look presentable. But this is Jill we're talking about. And you know that merely being presentable won't get you another date. And you do want another date, don't you?"

A text comes into Joe's phone and he looks at it. "She's already at the restaurant. I can't go change now. I've got to hurry up."

Jake nods. "Yeah, you're right. Just go. You can't change now. It's just too late."

Joe leaves without near the confidence he'd had before Jake put in his two cents.

Chapter 2.4: Intermittent Or Partial Reinforcement

Along with positive and negative reinforcement, we've got that in-between type of reinforcement that leaves us in limbo.

Jill waits outside the restaurant for Joe and Mandy waits with her. "How do I look, Mandy?"

"Um – you know, good. I guess." Mandy's still fuming a bit over the beach incident. But she's not one to straight-up lie to make anyone feel bad about how they look.

"You guess?" Jill runs her hand over her dress. "This dress isn't figure-flattering or what?"

"It's okay, sure." Mandy looks away, trying not to say anything too mean to her friend.

Jill fidgets nervously. "I wanted to look good. I mean, Joe's been after me to go out with him for as long as I can remember. Yesterday at the beach is the first time I really noticed the six-pack he's got going on. I mean, I never knew he was so muscular. I really wanted to look great for this date."

"And you do. Mostly." Mandy can't help herself. She's still angry about the beach incident and thinks Jill should get a taste of her own medicine. "I mean, the shoes are what bothers me about the outfit. Flats are so out right now."

Jill looks like she's panicking. "Can we switch shoes?"

Mandy shakes her head. "My feet are bigger than yours, remember?" They're actually the same size but last week Jill told Mandy that her feet were bigger than hers and Mandy knew she'd done it just to make her feel bad.

"I think I can fit in the sandals you've got on." Jill's looking like she's freaking out. "Come on, trade me. Please."

Mandy steps out of her shoes. "Sure. We can trade."

Smiling, Jill quickly trades shoes with her. But just as she gets them on, she sees Joe coming toward them. "Oh, he's here. You should go."

Mandy smiles. "Yeah, I'll go. Hey, just don't take the shoes off. I wore them to work the other day and they kind of stink like foot odor when I take them off. So, make sure you don't take them off or Joe's gonna think your feet stink. Have fun now."

Chapter 2.5: Punishment

Jill wasn't too thrilled with Mandy tricking her into trading ger for stinky shoes. She's out to punish her roommate for the transgression she committed.

Mandy has a favorite jacket she always wears, and Jill is about to make sure it can't ever be worn again. "I'm about to do a load of laundry, Mandy. Is there anything you want to be washed while I'm at it?"

Mandy's lying on the sofa, watching television. "On my floor are some dirty clothes. It would be awesome of you to throw them in with your things. Thanks."

Jill smiles the entire way to Mandy's bedroom. Picking up the clothes off the floor, she spots the jacket hanging on the back of a chair and grabs it too. Putting everything into the washer, she tosses in one brand new red towel. She's made sure there's nothing of hers that will get ruined, but Mandy's white jacket is soon to become pink.

Later, she puts all the laundry away, making sure to hang Mandy's jacket up in her closet. The stains will make it nothing more than trash now.

Jill smirks as she hisses to herself, "That's what she gets for leaving me with stinky shoes. Bet she doesn't pull anything like that again."

Chapter 2.6: Traumatic – One Time Learning

Jake goes into the bathroom not long after Joe comes home from his date. His roommate was happy with how the date with Jill had gone. So happy that Jake felt as if Joe was rubbing the connection he'd had with Jill in his face.

Jake had gone out with Jill on a few dates a few years back and considered Joe dating her to be not cool. Even though he'd told him it would be okay to go out with Jill, Jake hadn't thought the two would hit it off.

Jealousy is beginning to get to him, and he finds himself trying to figure out how to get between the two and end anything before it can really begin. Plus, teach Joe a lesson about friendship.

Joe had told him how much Jill had gone on and on about how muscular he was now and how great he looked since he'd let his hair grow out. So, Jake was about to fix one of those things about his roommate's appearance.

While he couldn't do a thing about his muscles, he could do a lot about his hair. Pouring out Joe's shampoo, he refilled it with a similar-looking thing, hair remover that women use to get rid of hair on their legs.

An hour later, after Joe gets out of the shower, Jake smiles as he hears his friend screaming. "Jake, what did you do?"

Jake is more than happy to let Joe know that he didn't approve of the transgression he'd made on their friendship. He goes to the bathroom, leaning casually against the doorframe as Joe pulls handfuls of dark hair off his head. "Yeah, that's for going out with a chick I used to see."

"You said it was okay, Jake!" Joe glares at him as he shakes the hair he's lost at him. "This is not funny!"

"No, you're wrong. It's hilarious. And the next time you even think about asking out a girl I used to date, you probably will recall this little lesson and not even ask me if it's okay. It's not. It never will be. And now you know, and I seriously doubt you will ever forget it."

Chapter 2.7: Lying By Omission

Jill had such a great time with Joe and is beginning to wonder why he hasn't called to make a second date. So, she calls him. "Hey, Joe. How's it going? I haven't heard from you in a week."

"Yeah, I've been busy," he replies.

"Okay." She feels a little worried that he didn't have as great a time as she did. "Are you going to be busy this weekend? I thought we might go out again if you're free."

"Um, I'm not sure. I'll have to get back to you."

"Joe, is everything okay?" She can't shake the feeling that he's not telling her something. "Did you not have as good a time as I thought you did?"

"Everything's fine. I'm just busy. I'll probably be busy for about a month, maybe a little longer than that." Joe's head looks like he's been in some type of an acid accident. Patches of hair are gone, and red, swollen areas are all over his head. He can't even go get his head shaved to make himself look any better. But he doesn't want Jill to know he's fallen victim to his roommate's terrible prank. Or whatever that was. "I'll call you when I get free, Jill. Bye."

Jill looks at the phone as she wonders what the heck happened.

Chapter 2.8: Denial

Later that week, Jill sees Jake, Joe's roommate, and a friend out at a club. "Hey, Jake. I talked to Joe. He's pretty busy huh?"

"I guess." Jake doesn't really want to talk to Jill about why Joe's not seeing her anymore.

Mandy comes up behind them. She's looking at Jake with a lot of judgment in her eyes. "I can't believe you did that, Jake! I just heard from one of Joe's co-workers that you put hair remover in his shampoo bottle and that he looks terrible. How could you?"

"I didn't do that!" Jake's not about to look bad in either of the women's eyes. "I think he had an allergic reaction to the shampoo. I don't know why he's blaming me."

Jill's jaw drops. "His hair! His gorgeous hair! It's gone?"

Mandy nods. "It will be soon. Joe's co-worker told me that the redness and swelling had gone down enough so that Joe could go get it shaved off now. He's going to be bald for some time now. And he sure did think it was you who did that, Jake."

"No way!" Jake looks at Jill. "You believe me, right? I wouldn't ever do anything like that, Jill. You know me better than that."

"Yeah, I guess you wouldn't do that to your friend. Poor Joe." As Jill chews on her lower lip, she thinks it's all for the best now that they didn't go out again. Part of her attraction to Joe was his awesome hair and now that's gone. "Too bad."

"Yeah, too bad." Jake thinks he's found a chance to get to see Jill again. "Hey, how about a drink, Jill? And maybe we can leave this loud club and go get some dinner somewhere nice and catch up. It's been a while since you and I went out together."

Now that Joe's out, Jill doesn't see why she and Jake can't reconnect. "Sure, Jake. That sounds like fun."

Chapter 2.9: Rationalization

Mandy can't believe that Jill would go out with the man who purposely messed up Joe's appearance.

She doesn't care what Jake has said, she knows he did what Joe's co-worker said he did.

She takes Jill by the hand, pulling her away from the creep. "Hey, before you go get that drink and leave, come with me to the ladies' room. You know how I hate to go alone."

"I'll be right back," Jill tells Jake. "Hey, get me a rum and coke. I'll meet you at the bar."

"Sure thing, babe." Jake turns to go to the bar.

Jill frowns at Mandy. "Mandy, what the heck are you doing?"

Pulling Jill to somewhere quieter where they can talk, she asks, "What the heck are you doing is the real question here? That jerk messed up Joe's appearance on purpose. You and Jake did use to date, Jill. It's no coincidence that Joe had suddenly lost his hair."

"I'm sure Jake isn't lying about that, Mandy. He's not a bad guy who would do something as sinister as that." Jill smiles as she thinks about when they used to date. "Jake's sweet when he wants to be."

Mandy knows what length some people will go to, to hurt someone. Her favorite jacket is at the bottom of a wastebasket thanks to Jill. "I think you're making rationalizations that aren't true just so you can see Jake again without feeling bad about doing it."

"You're wrong. And Joe had his chance. I called him just the other day to ask is he wanted to get together this weekend. He's the one who put me off. He could've told me about his condition, but he didn't." Jill put her hand on her hip as she felt like Joe lied to her by omission. "If Jake had done that to him, don't you think Joe would've told me that. He didn't say a word about not having any hair. He lied to me."

"I'm sure he was embarrassed." Mandy can't believe Jill would fall for what Jake's done.

"Whatever, Mandy. I don't think Jake did it. He said he didn't, and I believe him. So, I'll see you later – after Jake and I go out for dinner." Jill leaves Mandy speechless as she goes back to Jake.

Chapter 2.10: Minimization

When Jake gets back home, someone has called Joe to let him know about the date he and Jill went on earlier that night. "What the heck are you doing, Jake?"

"About what?" Jake takes off his jacket, tossing it on the sofa.

"You and Jill! You took her out to dinner." Joe's fuming mad. "You did this to me just so you could start seeing her again, didn't you?"

"No." Jake laughs. "That's a practical joke is what that is, Joe. And Jill and I accidentally ran into each other is all. It was just dinner between old friends, is all it was."

"Did you kiss her goodnight?" Joe smacks his fist against his palm.

Jake doesn't think he needs to let Joe in on everything he and Jill did. "No. It was just a couple of friends eating, Joe. No biggie."

"Did she ask about me?" Joe sits down, trying not to overreact.

"Sure. And I told her that you were getting over an allergic reaction you had to a new shampoo you used." Jake sat down too.

"So, you didn't take credit for what you've done?" Joe frowns at his friend.

Jake shakes his head. "Why would I want to make you look like a chump, Joe? No one needs to know about my little prank. But you seem to have told some people about work about it. Mandy told me about it. Don't worry, I glossed it over, so no one thinks bad about you."

"You mean that you glossed it over, so no one thinks you're a jerk," Joe says.

"Whatever, Joe. Let's watch some television and chill. No need for drama." Jake's happy that Joe seems to want to put everything aside too as he turns on the television.

Chapter 2.11: Selective Inattention Or Selective Attention

When Jill comes home, Mandy isn't speaking to her. "Aren't you going to ask me about how the date with Jake went, Mandy?"

Shrugging, Mandy says nothing.

Jill takes a seat on the sofa next to her friend. "Well, it went great. I forgot how great he and I get along."

Mandy stares at the television, seemingly ignoring Jill.

Jill can't figure out why Mandy would be mad at her for going out with Jake. "I don't know why you're giving me the cold shoulder, Mandy. It's not like you have feelings for Jake."

Mandy shrugs again without saying a word.

Jill knows that Mandy is just trying to make her feel bad for going out with Joe's roommate who she thinks put hair remover in his shampoo. "I know that you think Jake is a jerk who did something awful to his friend. I believe Jake though. I really don't think he did it."

Mandy sighs then gets up. "I'm going to bed."

"Wait," Jill says. "Can't we talk? I don't want you to be mad at me."

Mandy looks at her friend. "I'm not mad. Night."

But the way Mandy left the room lets Jill know Mandy doesn't approve of her seeing Jake and that bothers her.

Chapter 2.12: Diversion

With both their roommates upset with them, Jill and Jake aren't having happy homelives.

"Mandy's mad at me for going out with you," Jill tells Jake as they walk along the beach.

"Joe's mad at me too, for going out with you." Jake doesn't like the way things have turned out.

"You know what we could do, Jake?" Jill has come up with a great idea.

"Nope?" Jake's clueless about how to fix things.

"We can divert their attention away from us." Jill smiles as she's come up with the most perfect idea ever.

"And how are we to do that?"

"We can set them up together!" She thinks it's an awesome idea. "They'll be so busy with each other that neither will have time to think about you and me and what we're doing."

Jake likes the idea. "And then we can put all this negativity behind us and get back to a normal life. It's been a real bummer living with Joe since this whole thing began."

"Yeah, I know. Same with living with Mandy." Jill taps in a message for Mandy to meet her for lunch at a restaurant that's Mandy's favorite. "Send Joe to Mario's Bistro at one this afternoon and I'm sending Mandy there too. They'll meet up and start talking about us and how awful we are."

Jake taps in a message to Joe. "And then they'll stop talking about us and start talking about each other. It's a genius plan, Jill."

"I know. Diversion is the best!"

Key Takeaways

- Reinforcement. This comes in various forms. Positive. Negative. Partial. No matter which form one uses, there will be reactions that come from using reinforcements. And you can guide the reaction if you try to.

- Punishment. There are many ways to punish someone. From the cold-shoulder treatment to outright physical punishment, you can get your point across to others by using this tactic.

- Lying. Lying can be done in quite a few ways. Omitting things is the same as lying, even if some people don't believe this. Leading someone to think something that isn't true is lying. False words don't have to come out of your mouth for you to be a liar.

- Rationalization. Many people think that if you can come up with a reason for doing what you've done, then it makes it okay. It doesn't. If you hurt someone in any way, it's never okay.

- Diversion. This tactic is widely used to get one's self out of trouble or to get someone to get off a subject you'd rather not be on. Whatever the reason for using diversion, it's best to understand that the subject won't disappear, it will merely be taken off the table for a while – not forever.

Exercises

You want your spouse to take over a chore that is normally yours to do. Which tactic that you learned above would help you trick them into doing what you want them too?

You want to be the main attraction when someone you like walks up. But you've got a very attractive person with you who often steals all the attention without even trying to. What tactic that you learned from this chapter would help you gain the attraction you desire?

Is it right to use any of these tactics on other people?

Do you feel that you will be able to spot when someone is using any of the tactics you've learned in this chapter on you or someone you care about?

Chapter 3: Weapons Of Emotional Mass Destruction

Chapter 3.1: Introduction

Almost every person lies a few times each day. It might be as harmless as telling someone that they look good when they could look better. And it might be as harmful as telling someone that you love them when you really don't. Either way – we all lie.

When we lie to spare someone's feelings, we rarely feel guilty about doing it. Avoiding uncomfortable situations is the main reason people tell little white lies in the first place. And even big lies, like when a spouse tells their significant other that they're not cheating on them when they really are, it's meant to avoid the conversation at that time for whatever their reasons may be.

Those who lie about things that they know will have to be brought to light – such as the whole cheating thing – do so to avoid the fight that will ensue, the tears that will be shed, and the threats that will be made.

When it comes to lies, we are all procrastinators who somehow hope we will never have to deal with the lies we've told. Unfortunately, most of our big lies come to stare us in the face time and time again.

What seems a bit unfair is that the lie you told might be brought up again and again by whoever you told it to. This is to hurt you and make you feel bad all over again and it does nothing to fix the situation.

It's important, especially in strong and special relationships, that you apologize then refuse to do so again. This will let the other party know without a doubt that they will not be able to hold that over your head for the remainder of your life. After all, we all lie. That means they've lied to you too. They just haven't gotten caught yet.

Lies are one of the biggest weapons used in emotional destruction. It's easier to make something up about a person than to meticulously watch them until you find them doing something that you can use against them to destroy their emotions.

But there are quite a few techniques that one can use to destroy someone emotionally.

Chapter 3.2: Evasion

Who hasn't used evasion to give yourself space and time before dealing with someone who is trying to pin you down about something?

We'll use Sam and Beth Smith for an example. They're a couple who has been married for ten years. They really know one another and how to get around things and through things. But they also know how to hurt one another in ways that no one else knows how to accomplish.

One morning they wake up and Sam can't find his toothbrush. "Beth, did you move my toothbrush for some strange reason?"

"No, it should be where it always is, right next to your sink." She's in a hurry to get ready for work and jumps into the shower while her husband brushes his teeth.

Only he can't brush his teeth as he can't find his toothbrush. So, he hops into the shower with her. "Looks like it's disappeared, Beth. Shall I wash your back and you wash mine?"

"No." She turns around to put her back to him, not wanting him to see the front of her body. "You could've waited for me to get done. It never takes me long."

"We haven't showered together since I don't know when." He runs soapy hands over her back. Then he notices some red lines down the middle of her back. "Looks like you've managed to scratch your back somehow."

"Yeah, I must've bumped into a wall." She gets out of the shower. "I'll pick up a new toothbrush for you after work today."

"You don't have to do that. I'm sure I'll find mine. Or I can pick one up." He washes his hair, feeling like his wife is acting a little peculiar with all her hurrying. "Do you have an early meeting at work or something, hun? What's the huge rush?"

"Nothing. I just want to get there early it all. I'll see you after work, Sam. Have a good day." And then she's gone.

She's successfully evaded him and his questions about his toothbrush and the marks on her back. But at least he didn't see what she was really hiding and would have a devil of a time explaining away.

Chapter 3.3: Covert Intimidation

When people feel intimidated and the person doing the intimidating is doing it out in the open and not trying to hide anything, we can deal with that. It's the times when someone is intimidating you in a secretive way, or covertly, that is hard for us to deal with head-on. Mostly because if you ask the person if they're trying to intimidate you, they will lie to you and say, no.

Beth and Sam meet back at their house after work. Beth has a new toothbrush for her husband, but he bought one too. "I told you that I would get you one, Sam. Why'd you go out and buy one too?"

"I told you that you didn't have to do that. It's not a big deal. I'll put the one I bought away and use the one you got for me." He takes the toothbrush out of her hand and gives her a peck on the cheek. "Thanks anyway, Beth. The real mystery is where my old one is."

Huffing, she seems a little irritated. "It doesn't matter where it is. I might've tossed it in the trashcan for all I know. I've been in a rush lately, trying to set up this new deal at work. And it would be nice if I had some more help around here, to be honest." She pours herself a stiff drink then takes a seat on the sofa to try to chill out.

Sam comes back into the living room with a smile. "I can help out more. Tell what you'd like me to take on as far as chores are concerned, hun."

"Just take up the slack. That's all I'm asking from you. Just pick things up when you see them lying around. Just take out the trash when you see it needs to be done. Just do a load of laundry every once in a while. It won't kill you." She eyes him as he looks a little stunned by what she's said.

"I had no idea that I was slacking so badly." He pours himself a drink too. "I can do all that. It's not a problem at all."

Beth goes on, "It's just that I get overwhelmed by doing everything around the house. I'd like more free time. You know, the way you do. You've got your Tuesday night poker games with your buddies. I should get something like that too."

"You should. You can do whatever you want, Beth. I'm not stopping you." He takes a seat across from her, feeling that she needs a little space to vent.

"Maybe I will. Maybe I will get something to do on Tuesday nights too. I deserve that. I work hard. I keep this house immaculate. I do everything around here."

"Well, not everything, Beth. I've always taken care of the yard." Sam's feeling a bit defensive at it seems as if his wife is trying to make him feel bad. He's pulled his weight all these years, he has nothing to feel bad about. "Honey, are you trying to make me feel bad for some reason?"

"No. Why would I do that?" She takes a drink. "I mean, just because Sally from work says her husband has her a meal cooked each night when she gets home and he's got all the laundry done and put away, why would I want you to do all that? You're not a slave around here. We split the chores – mostly. And you. Well, you've got that bad back that makes it hard for you to do a lot of things. And you've got that weak stomach, so making anything I might like to eat wouldn't be a thing you could do either."

Sam's not sure how to feel. He wonders why he's feeling intimidated. Surely, Beth doesn't mean to be making him feel less of a person. She wouldn't do that to him. She's always been such a nice person and easy to get along and live with.

"Honey, I can't shake this feeling that something is bothering you." He tries to get to the heart of what's making her act so strangely.

"I'm just tired is all. Let's order pizza tonight. I just want to take a long, hot bath with a bottle of wine and relax. I want to think up what I'll do on Tuesday nights, now that I've got them free to do whatever I want to."

Chapter 3.4: The Guilt Trip

It's the following Tuesday, late that night, when Beth comes in from her night out. "It's two in the morning, Beth." Sam was worried sick when his wife didn't answer her phone when he called to see if she was okay. "Where in the world were you until this late hour?"

"You said I could do whatever I wanted to. And you didn't say I would have to answer a lot of questions either. What's the big deal? I'm home now, aren't I?" She goes to the bathroom, closing and locking the door behind her.

Sam isn't liking the vibe he's getting off her. She's been acting so odd lately. When she comes out, dressed in a nightgown that goes from her throat to her feet then walks right passed him and gets into their bed, he's got a terrible feeling. "You need to tell me where you were, Beth."

"Why? Don't you trust me, Sam? Haven't I been a trustworthy person all these years?"

"You have. But you've never stayed out so late and without giving me any reason for why that was." He crosses his arms over his chest. "So, where were you?"

"Out." She pulls the blanket up, tucking it all around her body. "You're kind of pissing me off right now. I don't ask you where you've been. Just go to bed.

You're treating me like a child, Sam. I don't like it at all."

"Well, I don't like not having a clue where my wife was tonight. So, there's that." He climbs into bed, beginning to feel a little guilty for how he's going on and on.

"I'm not a person who gets into trouble. Never have been. It would be nice if my husband of ten years could find it in his heart to just trust my word when I say that I've done nothing wrong. Geeze."

Feeling guilty for the scene he's made; Sam pulls the blankets up and tries to go to sleep.

Chapter 3.5: Shaming

After a week of Sam doing more chores around the house, he's proud of all he's taken on. "Here's the laundry. All folded and ready to be put away." He places the basket on the bed.

Beth pulls out a shirt of hers, holding it up. "It's wrinkled."

Sam looks at it and sees nothing wrinkled about the garment. "I think it looks fine."

She tosses it right back into the laundry hamper. "It's not fine. It's wrinkled and it doesn't smell right. Did you buy some cheap laundry detergent?"

"I used the same kind we've used for years. He goes to pull the clean shirt out of the dirty laundry basket she'd tossed it into. "I'll hang it up for you. Maybe then, if there are any wrinkles that I'm missing, they'll straighten out while hanging."

"Are you dumb or something?" Beth shakes her head. "That's not how wrinkles work. Just give it to me." She starts pulling the laundry that's hers out of the basket. "I'll rewash my clothes myself. I should've known better than to trust you with my clothes. I like to look a certain way. Apparently, you've never noticed that about me. There are many things that you don't notice about me."

Sam's confused and sits down on the bed as his wife yanks her clothes out of the basket of laundry he's just spent two hours doing. "Those clothes are fine, Beth. And what have I not noticed about you?"

"You never say that I'm your beautiful wife anymore. You haven't even noticed my haircut that I got a week ago. And how about my nails? I've been getting them done for a few months now and you've never even commented on them even once."

Cocking his head, he looked at her nails. "First, the nails. Those are what I've joked about being dragon-lady nails for years now. When I saw you'd done that to yourself, I thought it better not to say anything, rather than saying something that wasn't nice. And your hair is a bit on the short side — another thing I've told you that I don't like. But I didn't want to say anything mean, so I didn't say anything. And you're still my beautiful wife. I think I told you that only last week."

"I don't think so. So, you hate my hair and nails, is what you're saying?" She blinks back tears.

Now Sam feels ashamed of himself for saying the mean things he's said. "No. I – well, I.... Shit. I'm sorry. Forget I said anything." He grabs the basket of his clothes as she's taken all of hers out. "I won't try to do your laundry anymore. Sorry about the whole thing."

Chapter 3.6: Vilifying The Victim

"I'm sure that you are sorry, Sam." Beth takes her clothes and heads to the laundry room.

Sam watches her leave, then feels like she's the one in the wrong here, not him. "Wait. Are you not accepting my apology, Beth?"

"Just save it, Sam. It's not like you mean a word of it. You hate my hair and my nails. You don't care if I have to go to work in wrinkled clothes. It's like you want me to feel and actually be ugly." She slams into the laundry room, stuffing her clothes into the washing machine.

"You purposely got those awful fake nails and cut your hair like Peter Pan, Beth. And your clothes aren't wrinkled. You're making stuff up. And I think you're doing it just to try to make me feel bad. But guess what? It's not going to work. I go to work and have a strenuous day. Much more physical than what you do. And you say you need me to take up the slack around here and I do it without blinking an eye. And all I get in return is a wife who refuses to tell me where she goes on Tuesday nights until the wee hours of the morning and gripes that what I am doing, I'm not doing right."

Beth spins around, her eyes shining with unshed tears. "So, I'm the villain here? Me?" She gasps. "You tell me I look like Peter Pan and have dragon-lady nails and I'm the mean one?"

"Uh, yeah." Sam isn't going to stand there and take her crap one minute longer.

Chapter 3.7: Playing The Victim

Beth looks down as tears fall from her eyes. "If you really want to know what I've done the last couple of Tuesday nights, here it is, Sam." She looks up at him. "I sit in my car one street over. I don't do anything but try to enjoy my time alone, doing nothing. Would you like to know why that is?"

Sam isn't sure how to react to that. "Why is that, Beth?"

"Because I feel like you're always on my case. I feel like you run over me at every point that you can. I'm afraid of making you mad, Sam."

He looks away as he'd never meant to make her feel that way.

Chapter 3.8: Playing The Servant Role

The next few days are spent in awkward silence as Beth and Sam feel a rift forming between them. Beth has taken over all the chores, even the ones outside that Sam used to do.

Sam has no idea why she's doing everything all of a sudden. He's never seen her act this way and has no idea what to do. She beats him home from work each day and has everything done so there's nothing left for him to do. But she looks like she's wiped out from doing everything.

Sitting at the table, he's just not hungry and pushes the plate away. Beth, who is still eating, stops and puts down her fork. She jumps up and takes his plate away to wash it.

Sam grabs her wrist. "Beth, what are you doing?"

"Getting this out of your way." She looks into his eyes. "I'm sorry about how things have gone lately and want to make up for that."

"It's not all your fault, Beth. I have to take some of the blame too. And I can wash my own plate. I can do my own chores. Why are you mowing? Why are you weed-eating the sidewalk? You've never done those things and now you are, so why?"

"I'm sorry is why. I didn't mean to make you mad or upset you. I just want things to get back to normal. I don't know what else to do, Sam." She pulls out of his grasp. "Just let me do what I feel I have to do."

Sam's mind is a mess. He has no idea how things came to be this way. But he's got to fix it any way he can.

Chapter 3.9: Seduction

When Beth comes to bed later than night, she's wearing nothing but a smile. "So, how about we put this all behind us, Sam?" She climbs under the blanket with him, stroking his body as she kisses his neck.

But Sam isn't feeling right about anything. "Beth, I think we need to have a long talk, not just jump into having sex and thinking it will fix anything."

Stroking his stomach, she purrs, "Come on, babe. It'll work. You'll see. I'll do all the work. Let Momma take care of you."

But Sam isn't feeling it at all. He grabs her by the wrists. "I said no. You and I need to work some things out before we get intimate with each other again."

Chapter 3.10: Projecting The Blame

Beth's upset that Sam has stopped her advances. "I feel like I'm the only one trying here, Sam. You're not doing anything to fix this."

"That's mostly because I have no idea what broke in the first place. I'm confused, Beth." He sits up, wanting to work on what is wrong on their marriage, but not knowing what's wrong with it at all. We were fine up until about a month ago. So, what happened then?"

Beth sighs as she says, "You bought yourself that new truck is what happened. You've been acting different ever since that day."

"Me?" Sam doesn't think he's acted any different at all. "Are you kidding me, Beth?"

"You've always wanted a truck and when you got it, you started acting like some kind of a masculine jerk. Like you rule the roost around here. And I'm just the little lady you take care of. And I don't like where that's been leaving me."

Sam has no idea what she's talking about. "Yes, I've always wanted to buy a truck. But, Beth, I haven't been acting differently in any way. And I certainly don't think I rule the roost or that you're just some little lady. I respect you far too much to do that sort of thing."

"Then why have you need doing it?" She wipes her eyes as the tears have seeped out. "You never touch me anymore."

"The last time that I tried to touch you, you left the shower," Sam remembers the scratches that he's seen on her back that morning. "As a matter of fact, you were acting very weird that morning. You made sure not to turn around to face me. Is there something I should know, Beth? Have you been messing around with someone?"

Chapter 3.11: Feigning Innocence

"I don't know what you're even talking about. I don't remember doing that at all. When did we take a shower together?" Beth asks as she looks at Sam with big brown eyes.

"That morning when my toothbrush went missing is when we did that. I'm finding it hard to believe that you can't recall that." Sam's feeling very prickly as he knows his wife is lying to him. "So, why would you lie about remembering something like that? Is it because you didn't get those scratches the way you said you did? Did someone put those scratches on your back, Beth?"

Chapter 3.12: Feigning Confusion

"What scratches?" Beth looks confused. "Sam, what are you talking about? I don't remember having scratches on my back. Why are you making this stuff up about me? What have I ever done to you?"

Sam is sure he's onto something. "You're not fooling me, Beth Smith. I will get to the bottom of this, come hell or high water. You should fess up now and save yourself the trouble that'll come along with me having to search out this man you've been cheating on me with."

"Sam, I don't understand, babe. I really don't. I would never cheat on you. The shower never happened. I think that must've been a dream, babe. You've been working too hard. That's why I took on all the chores, so you could rest and get better." She shakes her head, looking like she just doesn't understand anything. "Sam, I'm so confused, babe."

But all Sam can think is – *Sure you are.*

Key Takeaways

- In emotional mass destruction there is the victim and the villain.
- Using techniques to undermine the victim's senses and emotions, the villain can turn the whole situation around to make the victim

seem as if he was the one who has done wrong to her.

- As with all destruction, people on both sides can get hurt by the fallout.

Exercises

Your spouse comes in with some strange marks on their body that raises your internal instincts. Do you ask questions? Or do you turn into a private eye and find the answers you seek by sneaking around and spying on them?

If you get caught spying, do you confess or lie?

If you ask your spouse in a straightforward way about the marks, do you also let them know if you think they're lying? Why? Or why not?

Is it ever okay to twist things around to put the blame on someone else when you know that it is you who have done wrong?

Chapter 4: The Subtle Art Of Getting What You Want

Chapter 4.1: Introduction

Persuasion isn't always easy to do. The people you want to persuade have the right of free choice. There will be other options they can take, leaving your option behind.

We see it in advertising all the time. You have so many different types of products to choose from that it makes picking just one a difficult task. So the makers of all products on the market today must persuade you to buy only their product.

Think about all the different types of soda there are in the market today. Each company has its own unique way of persuading the drinkers of soda to buy their drink. "It's fizzier than all the rest."

Who wouldn't want the fizziest of all the sodas?

Maybe someone with tummy issues.

So, there's another company that has thought about that and they try to persuade buyers in another way. "Our soda is the smoothest of them all."

Yes, a smooth taste is always good except if you're a kid who likes to astonish his senses. Then the company has to persuade that kid to buy their soda. "Your taste buds won't know what hit 'em when you drink our soda."

There are those who don't want any caffeine in their soda. So, the company has an idea to persuade those soda drinkers. "All the taste and none of the caffeine of our competitors' sodas."

But what if someone wants more caffeine? Companies had to come up with how to persuade those people too. "Your morning routine just got better with Hyper-speed soda with three times the caffeine of any other brand."

With so many choices out there, persuasion has never been more important. Learning how to get people to buy your product, vote the way you want them to, or think that way you need them to think, is an essential piece of knowledge everyone needs in this day and age.

Chapter 4.2: Brandishing Anger

More so used in politics, brandishing anger is a technique that's meant to hit you at your core.

Take this example:

Mack is running for president of the United States. And he's angry with the current president. So, he needs you to get angry with him, so you'll vote for him and not the man he's so angry with. "You can't sit back and just allow him to keep on running our country into the ground! You've got to do something, and it has to happen right now! There is no time to wait! How will you look your children in their little faces, knowing that you never even tried to make their futures better by voting for me, the best man to take over the White House?"

As you can see here, he's mad and he's letting you know that he and your kids will be so mad at you if you don't vote for him and get the other guy out of office. He's using anger to persuade you to do as he wants you to.

Chapter 4.3: Bandwagon Effect

Mack's no fool either. He didn't get to where he is by being unprepared. So, he's brought along his bandwagon to help persuade you further to cast your vote for him. "Look who I have here with me today. My elite supporters. You all know Josh from his many movie roles that have won him many Academy Awards. And who can forget about Manny's Pulitzer? He's a staunch supporter that anyone would be admired for following. We've got an awesome group here, people. It would make us all very happy to have you all join us in this great endeavor. Come, join us, the nation's best and brightest leaders."

Now, who wouldn't want to join that nation's best and brightest? And Josh, the Academy Award-winning actor is so handsome too. Who knows, maybe you'll end up working at a rally together if you join team Mack for the presidency?

Chapter 4.4: Lying

Pretty much every politician anywhere has been accused of lying at one time or another. That's only because they've all lied at one time or another.

As I pointed out before, we all lie at least a few times each day. If you're a politician who is talking as much as you can to get into the office you're seeking, then you probably lie a heck of a lot more than the rest of us do.

So, getting caught in a lie isn't a thing that actually worries you. You know it will happen and you're prepared for that day.

A reporter raises his hand in the crowd in front of Mack. "Yes, Robbie the reporter?"

"Mack, you said in the last rally that you've been married for ten years. But I have done my research and that's not true at all. See, you were married for a matter of six months to a woman named Pam when you were fresh out of high school. If you add the time you've been married to your current wife, Arlene, to the time you were married to Pam, you've got eleven years in all."

Mack is ready to admit his lie. "Yes, you caught that, did ya, Robbie. Yes, I was briefly married to my high school sweetheart. We're still great friends by the way. And the reason that I don't count that time as being married is that – if you would've researched just a tad bit more – you would've found that that marriage was annulled, making it not count."

"Oh," Robbie the reporter says with a bit of embarrassment. "Sorry about that, Mack. Go on, you were saying?"

Mack was ready with his rebuttal and never even blinked an eye when confronted.

Chapter 4.5: Using Guilt

Who doesn't know that using guilt to get what you want actually works? Anyone can pull this off too. From a little kid to an elderly person, we all know how to use this great tactic when we need to.

It's like we were all born with this innate sense to help us get the things we want.

Take Johnny for instance. Johnny is six years old and he would love nothing more than to get a video game system like the ones his friends have. "Aw, come on, Dad. All the guys have one."

"Those things cost a fortune, Johnny," Dad exclaims as he puts down his newspaper. "Plus, you have to be careful with them or they can break. The last thing I want to see is something that cost me a ton of money, lying broken in the trash bin. So, for the tenth time, no. You can't have one of those things yet. You're just too young for that kind of responsibility."

Johnny puts on the puppy dog eyes as he holds his hands in front of him. "But, Dad, I will be the most careful I've ever been with anything in my entire life. If you give me that one thing, then I will never ask for another thing again as long as I live."

"Yeah?" His father grins. "So, if I get you this machine, you won't ask me for a car when you're sixteen? You won't ask me to rent you a tuxedo when you have your high school graduation? You won't ask me for even one Christmas or birthday present? And how about Easter and Halloween? You won't ask me to buy you a costume so you can go trick or treat with your friends and your brothers and sister? You won't ask me for an Easter basket so you can put the eggs you find in it?"

"Are you serious right now, Dad?" Johnny can't believe his father would go that far.

"Sure, I'm serious right now, son. You've got to think about what you say to me. Saying that if I get you this one thing then I won't have to get you anything else, just isn't true." Johnny's dad sees a lesson here. "Although you don't mean to, you're intentionally lying to me. And that just to drink their bottlehurts, son."

Johnny can tell that something is shifting in their roles within this very important conversation and he can't let that happen. "Well, I am sorry. I didn't know that I was lying to you. I wouldn't do that to you, Dad. But you should know that my friends are the same age and they all have gaming systems that their parents all trust them with. That makes me feel like you think they're smarter than me."

Johnny's dad never meant to make his son feel that way. "Son, I didn't mean to make you feel bad. But, maybe their parents just aren't as aware of the fact that their kids are too young to be trusted not to break such an expensive item. I'm sure one of them will break their game very soon."

"What?" Johnny's eyes bug out. "You would wish that on my friends, Dad? How could you? I was just asking if you could find it in your heart to get me a gaming system. I never thought you would turn on my poor friends like this. I'm sorry I even brought it up to you now that I know how you are. I would never - not ever – wish anything bad for your friends, Dad. Like what if I said that I know that soon your buddy next door will wreck that sports car he just bought? How would that make you feel?"

"Well, pretty good, actually. That guy is too old to be driving a Corvette."

"Shame on you, Dad. Shame, shame, shame." Johnny wags his finger at his father. That man deserves that car. He's worked his whole entire life and all he wanted was to get to buy himself a car like that before he died. Shame on you, Dad."

Johnny's father is left dumbstruck. And he begins to reflect on himself. "You know what?"

"What, Dad?" Johnny crosses his arms over his chest as he waits to see what his father has to say.

"Maybe I'm saying no to you out of jealousy. I never got a game system until I was old enough to buy my own. Go get your shoes on. I'm taking you to get one right now."

Johnny runs off, shouting how much he loves his father. And not an ounce of guilt is felt by the kid for playing his father like that either.

Chapter 4.6: Persuasion

We've all heard these words, 'Can I persuade you?'

Me, being me, I always say back, "No, you may not?" But I'm a real piece of work, so anyone who knows me expects that to come out of my mouth.

But if you really want to know how to get what you want, then you will leave out the actual words that let the person know that you are about to mentally manipulate them into doing what you want them to.

Andy was looking for a new car. He knew that he wanted a great deal and would be taking the cheapest car on the lot that very day. And the thing was that the salesman knew Andy was going to leave there with a car that very day because Andy had made the mistake of telling him that.

So, Leo, the salesman needs to make more commission from the sale that the cheapest car there won't bring him. Persuasion begins to play. "Yes, that is our cheapest car, Andy. And it's an okay car. But let me ask you this. Will this car last a whole year before it needs lots of expensive repairs, costing you even more money down the road to keep it running?"

It sounds to Andy like Leo is trying to give him good advice. "So, what are you saying, Leo? Should I look at something that will last longer?"

"Now, that is all up to you. I ain't one of these pushy salesmen like the rest of the guys here on the lot. I just like to help my customers get the best deal they can for the money they got."

"And I would appreciate your sage advice, Leo." Andy feels lucky that he got such a great man to help him buy his first car.

That's another thing Leo knows about Andy since he told him that as well. "Being that this is your first car, Andy, I'd hate for you to get into something with nothing but problems. Now, let me show you what I think would work for you. And mind you, it will cost a bit more, but I've got a humdinger of a great deal for you on how you can pay this car out."

Andy's surprised and pleased. "Do you mean that you can get me financed, Leo?"

"In-house is our specialty here at Gotta Have it Motor Company. You can just give us what you came here with as the down payment and then I'll write up a finance deal for you, and you'll only be charged fifty percent interest."

"Fifty sounds high to me." Andy is seeing a downside to Leo's idea.

"You should always ignore the interest charge. It's not like it will ever affect your relationship with your car. And your payment will still be affordable," Leo advises him.

"For how long, are we talking here?" Andy had to ask, knowing that he's already got some bills to pay out of the paycheck he earns from flipping burgers down at Quickie Burger.

Waving his hand as if waving away some pesky mosquitos, Leo lets him know it's not so long, "Sixty months is all." Leo knows when you use the smaller unit of time of a month over the larger unit of time of saying a year, then you can hook people a lot more easily. "Sixty payments is all you will have to make to become the owner of this car." He opens the door of a gently used Chevy Camaro. "Look at this beauty. Now, this is what every eighteen-year-old wants to be driving. Am I right?"

"I can't afford this." Andy knows this is just too good to be true. "The payments will be way too high."

"You tell me what's more important to you and I'll help you find the right car for you." Leo taps his chin as he seems to be thinking. "Is it more important to you to get great gas mileage, or pay a lower payment on a car?"

"Um, well, both kind of." Andy isn't sure where the guy is going with this.

"Okay, well then you should know that this car gets the best gas mileage out of all the cars we have on this lot right now. So, you might pay a little bit more per month but in the end, you will save it at the pumps." Leo smiles as if he's solved the kid's problems.

"And what happens if I can't come up with the payment at times?" Andy had to wonder about that.

"Not a problem in the least, Andy. See, we'll just come to pick the car up and bring it back here, keeping it here until you can pay if that doesn't take too long. We can't keep something sitting her forever. And lots of people will be ogling this yellow beauty. You probably wouldn't want to miss any payments and risk someone else buying your little beauty."

Andy looks at the sports car. "It is a beauty. And my girlfriend would love it if I came to pick her up in this."

"Oh, you will have her eating out of the palm of your hand if you take this thing to pick her up in. Eating out of the palm of your hand! So, how about a test drive?"

"Man, I shouldn't." Andy's getting a little apprehensive about the whole thing. He never went there to get himself wrapped up in payments. He wanted to pay cash for a car and get going.

Pulling the keys to the car out of his pocket, Leo tosses them to Andy. "Come on, let's take a spin. You drive. I'll show you how the stereo works while you take us on a cruise. You can see how the ladies on the street react to you behind the wheel of this beast."

"Yeah. What could a little drive hurt?"

The answer to that is well known by most of us. It can make you fall in love so hard with a car that paying only sixty payments doesn't sound so hard for you to do. You have to work for love, and you love this car. All thanks to Leos' ability to use persuasion without you ever knowing a thing about it.

Chapter 4.7: Dissuasion

As easy as it is to use the power of persuasion, it's also easy to use the power of dissuasion. For this little scene, we will pick up with Andy and Leo right where we left off.

When the two got back to the lot, there sat Andy's father, waiting for them to return. He's all smiles as they get out of the car. "Hey, Andy. I noticed how long it was taking you and thought I'd come on up here to help you make a decision, buddy."

"Well, Dad, I think I've made on. This is it. This is my first car." Andy pats the hood of the car that has a bit of smoke coming out of it.

"What's that smoke about?" Andy's dad asks Leo.

"Leo, sir." He extends his hand to Andy's father. "Great to meet ya."

"Ray." He shakes the salesman's hand. "So, the smoke? What's up with that?"

"I think it's a little oil that might've spilled while we were filling it up. That's all. With the swipe of a cloth, it'll be nothing."

"Let's pop the hood, shall we. I wanna get a gander at my boy's first-ever engine." Ray reaches into the driver's side, popping the hood.

The smoke really billows out as he opens the hood. Andy waves the smoke out of his face. "Wow, there must be a whole bunch of oil that spilled when you were filling it, Leo."

"Yeah, I guess so." Leo puts his hands into his pockets, rocking back and forth, as he tries to figure out how he's going to persuade the kid's old man into letting him buy the heap of crap.

"Well, Andy," his dad says. "I think the first thing you should ask here is why oil is having to be put into this car in the first place. You know, ask if there's a leak or something."

"Oh, yeah." Andy looks at Leo. "So, is there a leak?"

"Not that I'm aware of." Leo knows there's one. "We like to make sure all the oil levels are topped off each morning is all. One of the mechanics must've just spilled some on the engine is all. I can have them get that all cleaned up while we get to the paperwork. Not a problem at all."

"Well, hold up there, Leo," Ray says. "I'm sure Andy has more he'd like to ask you before you put in too much effort on this deal. Right son?"

"Um, yeah sure, Dad." Andy looks around the car and finds something a little odd. "Um, why is the paint on the inside of the car door red and the car is yellow on the outside, Leo."

"Paint job, obviously." Leo knows the car has been in a wreck. It was totaled by the insurance company and his boss bought it at a salvage yard. "Guess the last owner liked yellow more than red. No biggie. Lots of people paint their cars."

Andy looked at his father. "Is that right, Dad?"

"I've had ten cars in my life," his dad says. "Never painted any one of them. See, son, a paint job can also mean there has been damage to the car. Let's take a look at the inside of the car for a minute."

Andy pointed out a torn seat cover in the back. "I saw this, but Leo said a little needle and thread could stitch this up."

"Yeah, so why haven't they done that if that's the case?" Ray asked. "Have you asked to see the vehicle's maintenance record?"

"Didn't know I could ask that." Andy turned to Leo. "Can I see that?"

"You sure could," Leo said with a smile. "If the owner who sold it to us had left it in the car. Sorry. But we can get to the paperwork if you're ready."

The look in his father's eyes told Andy that as much as he wanted the car, his dad thought it was a bad deal. "You know, Leo. I think I'm going to hold off. I'll save a little more money so I can buy something else outright a little later. I really don't want payments."

Ray claps Andy on the back. "I think you're right about doing that, son. Damn proud of you. You do have a good head on your shoulders."

Leo has to do something. He hadn't sold a car in days. And he's not about to miss out on making at least a little. "Well, what about the first car I showed you. We can still do that deal. That's a cash out the door price I gave you for that."

Andy looks at his Dad who once again, gives him that look that says it's a bad idea. "Naw. Thanks, Leo. I'll see you around."

Using the power of dissuasion, Andy's father has saved Andy tons of car trouble in the future.

Chapter 4.8: Bribery

There is no parent in the world who hasn't used bribery to get their kids to do something.

Mother's beg their kids to eat their vegetables. "Come on, Lacy, eat your peas. They're good for you."

"No! Yucky," the three-year-old screams as she shakes her head.

So, Mom resorts to bribery. "If you take one bite of these peas, then we will go down to the ice cream shop and you can get any flavor that you want."

With wide eyes, Lacy opens her mouth and Mom has won. Or has she?

Chapter 4.9: You Scratch My Back – I'll Scratch Yours

This may have come from caveman times. I can see one man having a terrible case of the fleas in the bushy hair covering his back. He can't reach the itch and has to go ask another caveman who seems to have an itch he can't scratch too.

In so many grunts and hand gestures, he gets the other caveman to see that they can both get their itches taken care of if they work together.

This technique for getting what you want has evolved quite a bit. And like anything else, it's been used for evil more than a time or two. Politicians use this technique on a daily basis nowadays.

Chapter 4.10: Blackmail

Blackmail is a technique that can actually go from something a little bad to do to a person to something that is considered to be a crime and a punishable offense.

So, you can see a lame blackmailing scheme here. Jana is taking a nap and when her kid doesn't let her sleep, she resorts to blackmailing her. "Hey, you better go lay down and take your own nap or I'll tell your daddy that you didn't take it and he won't take you for ice cream after dinner."

And then you have a criminal offense. "So, you will say that you murdered that man, or I will kill your entire family, Frank. Got it?"

There are many shades of grey with this tactic for getting what you want.

Chapter 4.11: Ultimatum

I don't know about you, but when some idiot thinks they're going to give me an ultimatum and I'll fall for it, I leave them empty-handed.

The whole, you can do this or this and nothing else scam is a real turn off. But so many people fall for it, that it keeps on happening.

Dave is about to dish out a couple of things Linda can do. "So, you can clean the house and I won't scream and yell at you, or you can clean the house with me screaming and yelling at you."

Now, a smart person would give him a quick answer to that. "Or you can clean your own damn mess cause it was you who made it in the first place. I'll be next door, watching television with the neighbors. Let me know when you're done."

Chapter 4.12: Hidden Agenda

The hidden agenda strategy can be pulled off without anyone being the wiser of this nifty little trick of getting what you want. The key here is not to let too much get out about what you really want.

"So, I've got this golf club set that's just taking up space in my closet. Would you like to have it, Wilma? You could give it to your husband as a gift."

"Won't your husband be angry that you gave away his clubs, Lola?" Wilma's not sure she wants to be involved in that mess. "I don't want Chester to be playing golf and have Harry come at him like a tiger when he sees him using his clubs."

"Oh, that won't happen. Harry knew I was gonna clean out the closet. He won't be mad at Chester." But Lola knows that Harry loves those clubs and he would hate for her to give them away.

"I don't know. I don't want to get in the middle of anything bad." Wilma knows that the couple has a tumultuous relationship.

"Well, I'm gonna give them to someone, or I'm gonna put them in a dumpster somewhere. Either way, give them to your husband or not. I'm getting my closet cleaned out." Wilma is set on getting rid of the clubs her husband loves so much.

"Well, if you're just gonna throw them out, then sure I'll take them. Chester will be pretty happy with a free set of clubs." She's feeling okay with taking them now that she knows they would've been turned into trash.

Lola takes the clubs worth thousands of dollars and gives them to her friend. "There you go. Now I've got to clean up the rest of the closet. Thanks, Wilma. Bye now." Lola has more she has to get rid of but didn't want to ask her friend to take too many of her husband's things or she might get suspicious.

Lola had an agenda. She'd caught Harry cheating on her and now she's going to get rid of the things he loves the most, starting with the golf clubs and ending with her.

Key Takeaways

There are many ways to get what you want. Each tactic above can be used in both good and bad ways.

- Using Anger.
- Getting people on your bandwagon.
- Lying.
- Using guilt.
- Using persuasion and dissuasion.
- Lying to get what you want.

- Bribing others to get what you want from them.
- Scratching backs to get yours scratched too.
- Using blackmail against others.
- Having hidden agendas.
- Giving others ultimatums.

It's up to you how you use these techniques.

And now you can spot them when they're being used on you.

Exercises

You find someone flattering you for absolutely no good reason as you aren't dressed up in any way take and you actually look kind of tacky. What do you do?

Someone you know asks you to do something that you consider to be immoral. When they tell you that you will do it or they will do something really bad to you or someone else, what is that called?

If you have a reason you want someone to do something, that is called having a what?

You come home to find the place a wreck and ask your kids to clean up their mess. They give you a lot of trouble doing it. Then you tell them that they will get to go to the movies if they get the house cleaned up. What is that tactic called?

Chapter 5: Sneaky Ways Of Covert Hypnosis

Chapter 5.1: Introduction

Often done while having what might seem to be a normal conversation, covert hypnosis – by definition – means that a person is being hypnotized without realizing what's going on.

While this might bother or upset some people, it's important to know the facts. The fact is that we were all covertly hypnotized while we were kids and our brains were still forming. Our parents and anyone with any authority over us and our learning experiences did this to us, not knowing that they were actually hypnotizing the children they loved. And we've all done it to our own children and any we have authority over as well.

We put our ideas and expectations into their brains over and over again. If you think about it for a moment, you will understand how this whole thing works. You might've heard your mother say something like, "We are Baptists, and we believe in that religion and that one alone."

You were never given a choice about what religion you were - it was decided for you. But as you grew up, you found yourself truly believing the way you'd been told to.

But many of us began to hear things from others and see things on television that had us questioning things. It was when our brains matured that we used our own mind to make decisions. And as long as you still use your own mind and don't just believe whatever anyone tells you, then you won't fall victim to covert hypnosis.

Chapter 5.2: Conversational Hypnosis

This is by far the most common type of covert hypnosis that anyone will encounter. It's done on all platforms too – social, media, advertising – you name it, this technique has been and is currently being used.

Chapter 5.3: Keywords That Disengage The Conscious Mind

To get a person to stop thinking clearly on their own, some words help the covert hypnotist to shut down the conscious mind. Using words like *imagine* and *relax* are just a couple.

Here is a whole list of keywords for you to use or be aware of them being used on you.

Envision.

Visualize.

Picture.

Dream.

See.

Think.

Conceive.

Invent.

Concoct.

Make up.

Dream up.

Make-believe.

Think of.

Suppose.

Expect.

Assume.

Presume.

Guess.

Understand.

Diminish.

Reduce.

Lower.

Ease.

Unwind.

Calm down.

Slow down.

Let go.

Loosen up.

Lighten up.

Settle Down.

Rest.

Take it easy.

Put your feet up.

Chill out.

Lie down.

Loosen.

These words are powerful enough to stop a person from their present train of thought and put them in a state that makes it much easier to get into their minds and warp them in the ways you wish to.

Chapter 5.4: Visualization

Much like a writer who wants to take their readers on a real journey in their minds, words can be used to make you visualize things.

When someone asks you to see something that could be, they are putting a picture into your head, trying to get you to do what they want you to. Seeing is believing after all – even if you're just seeing it in your mind.

Chapter 5.5: Ambiguity

As defined by Wikipedia - ambiguity is a type of meaning in which a phrase, statement or resolution is not explicitly defined, making several interpretations plausible. A common aspect of ambiguity is uncertainty. It is thus an attribute of any idea or statement whose intended meaning cannot be definitively resolved according to a rule or process with a finite number of steps.

If this confuses you, then you are now witnessing ambiguity at its finest — politicians bank on this kind of thing. How man speeches have you listened to that when finished you have no idea what the heck all that talk was all about?

Beware this type of speech as it puts your brain into a semi-conscious state as it tries to find something of interest or importance within all the words that the speaker is spewing or droning on about.

Chapter 5.6: Vagueness

Being vague is what most people do when they have no intention of committing to anything. When someone says maybe – most people take that as a no. When someone says, might – most people take that as a no.

There are various ways of being vague. You can be trying not to tell someone the truth about something. Let's say that Sandra has a new hair cut and you don't care for it. But she asks you if you like it and you're stuck.

"Um, well, it's very different for you, isn't it?" You might vaguely ask.

When someone doesn't answer you outright, they're being vague with you to avoid something. Maybe it's to avoid hurting your feelings. So you might not want to push it and just accept the fact that not everyone is going to agree with everything you do or say.

Chapter 5.7: I'm Not Going To Tell You

I'm sure you've heard someone tell you that they aren't going to tell you something but then they tell it to you right away.

Take this little sentence for example. "I'm not going to tell you to eat more chicken, but research shows that you need to eat more chicken."

This is so in your face, that we sometimes miss the fact that we're being directed to something. When someone acts as if they aren't telling you what to do, that disengages the mind, then they enter what they want you to do to reengage it in the way they want you to.

Think about how many things you've never wanted until someone told you something great about it, after telling you that they aren't going to tell you what to do.

It is truly crazy how our minds work.

Chapter 5.8: Embedded Commands

These simple statements are mixed into about a paragraph worth of words. It's most often used in advertising to get people to make a purchase that they wouldn't otherwise make.

Take this example of embedded commands that will be written in bold so you can spot them.

I won't tell you to **buy my product** because I respect you and believe that you have the right to make your own decisions. What I will do is let you know enough about my product so you can **think about my product**, imagine what it can do for you. And then you can make your own decision to **buy my product**.

You can clearly see how your mind is being taken over. You are expected to buy this product because you are told twice to do it and once to think about it. In the end, you most likely will want to take a chance and buy it since the sales technique seemed not to be too forceful and off-putting.

Chapter 5.9: Cause And Effect

Cause and effect are powerful tools in the mind game business. Some scientists believe that people can see cause and effect even when it doesn't really exist.

If someone tells you that you broke a rule and so you have to be punished – that is cause and effect. But what makes their rule your rule?

Maybe walking on the left side of the road is what they're saying you did that broke a rule that you didn't know they had. And when they tell you that the punishment for breaking that rule is to pay a fine of a hundred dollars, you are startled, stunned, then outraged.

But chances are you will pay the fine and swear never to go back to that place again. You saw cause and effect when it didn't really exist. Because you didn't make sure there really was a rule like that and the conman got your money.

Be sure that you can clearly see that there is a real cause to affect you before you accept it as a fact.

Key Takeaways
Now you can spot things you might not have been able to before.

- Conversation hypnosis is the most commonly used form of hypnosis.

- Visualization is used to make you see something that's not there or tangible.

- Ambiguity is the art of talking in circles that lead to nowhere.

- Vagueness is when one skirts around an issue without giving their real opinions or answers.

- Telling someone that you won't tell them what to do, then tell them what to do anyway.

- Embedding commands to hide the fact that you want to tell someone to do something.

- Cause and effect, knowing when there is a real one and a fake one.

Exercises

If someone begins talking to you, using any of the keywords designed to disengage your conscious mind, what will you do to counteract this?

The next time you hear someone say that they aren't going to tell you something then do, what will you do?

If someone tells you that you have to suffer the effect that your actions have caused, what will you do about that?

Are you going to use any of these techniques to try to get others to do what you want them to do? And why or why not?

Chapter 6: Hostile Mind Takeover

Chapter 6.1: Introduction

Brainwashing. A pretty scary word, right?

Thankfully, it's not a thing most of us have to worry about. True brainwashing takes time and the subject has to be kept in a situation that breaks them in ways one can't be broken unless held captive.

Wikipedia defines this best - Mind control is also known as brainwashing, coercive persuasion, mind abuse, thought control, or thought reform and all these words refer to a process in which a group or individual systematically uses unethically manipulative methods to persuade others to conform to the wishes of the manipulator, often to the detriment of the person being manipulated.

So let's see what all is involved in this lengthy process, shall we?

Chapter 6.2: Repetition

You did it. You did it. You did it. If you're seated in a small room you are locked in and cannot leave, escape by falling asleep, or ignore the person saying this over and over, the chances are that you will finally admit to something even if you didn't do it.

If it will shut the person up, you would agree to anything.

Annoying someone often gets them what they wanted.

Being annoying might seem like it shouldn't work. And it won't if the other person can get away from the annoying person. But we can't always get away from people who are making us crazy by asking things or saying things over and over again.

Even something that is making the same noise over and over or continuously will have you changing your mind, no matter how well it was made up, just to shut them up.

Think about your baby who is crying in their crib because they don't want to go to sleep alone. They've been fed, bathed, burped, put a dry diaper on and everything should be fine for them just to drink their bottle and go night-night.

Only you loved them so much when they were first born that you just couldn't stand to lay them down after they fell to sleep in your arms. No, you held them and rocked them as you gazed down at their darling little sleeping face.

But then the months passed, and the baby got bigger and you felt like the time had come to let them learn how to go to sleep on their own. But that baby doesn't want to do that. And that baby has a lung capacity to rival the best swimmers on the planet. And it will continue to cry, scream, and throw everything it can until you give in.

And you will give in. We all do. The sound can drive a person crazy and you can't walk away and leave your baby all alone so you can get away from the sound.

Bad people took this innate nature of people and learned how to use it against them. They learned that if you removed the person's capability to leave your presence, then you could effectively pound what you want into their heads.

Most people don't have any good intentions when they set out to do this. And what you really need to watch out for are the authorities. They take you to a small room – the interrogation room. This is a room that you aren't supposed to get up and walk out of. They have you trapped and sometimes they do lock the door to make sure you don't leave.

What you need to know – **Do not talk without having a lawyer present!!!**

No matter what they say or do or try to get you to say or do, don't do a thing except say that you need to get a lawyer before you say a word.

First – they have already taken away your ability to leave their presence. This gives them the time to keep repeating things to you and manipulating your mind. And we all now know that most of us can be made to think things that aren't true. Our minds are more susceptible than any of us really knew!

Chapter 6.3: Imitation

When we imitate someone's body language and some of the words they use often, we make them think we are like-minded. People like it when others believe the way they do, like the things they do and have the same types of goals that they do.

You have to make the person think you have their best interest at heart if you are to truly brainwash them.

Chapter 6.4: Saying Don't Instead Of Can't

You can trick your mind into thinking that you came up with the idea that you don't want to do something rather than that you can't.

Why?

We hate to be told what to do as children and adults. It's just part of being human.

If you are on a strict diet and someone asks if you'd like a donut, you might say that you can't have one because you're on a diet. But that might make your brain spark up and it will tell you that you can't be told what to do by anyone.

So, you trick your mind. If asked if you want a donut, you can say, "No, I don't want one. Thanks though." That way it won't wake up that part of your brain that thinks it shouldn't be told why it can and can't do.

Chapter 6.5: Rituals

Rituals help us to accept things. Back in your school days, you most likely had a morning ritual that helped you get to school. Without a ritual, you would most likely miss a lot of school as you might just wake up and think you would rather not go that day and roll over and go back to sleep.

So, your parents instilled a ritual to help you get up and get to school. The alarm goes off in your parents' room and you begin to stir as you hear it. Your mother comes to the side of your bed, kissing your cheek. "Time to wake up for school, honey. I'll get breakfast going while you hop in the shower, then brush your teeth and hair, then get dressed and come to the breakfast table."

So, you rolled out of bed, groaning and maybe even complaining a little, "Aw, Mom, I don't want to go to school today. Can't I just stay sleeping?"

"Don't be silly. Now off to the shower, young man."

After a shower, you feel more awake and as each ritual is completed you wake up a bit more and now you're on the routine, moving right along as you do each day.

And this routine sets you up for having a job one day where you will develop something similar to get you into the right mind frame to do whatever it is you need to do.

Chapter 6.6: Saying Excited Instead Of Afraid

Another brain trick is using excited instead of afraid. Rollercoasters can be used for this example. You're standing in the long line for hours and your mind can really mess with you in that amount of time.

You start to shake as you hear the screams coming from the ride you're about to get on. "I better not go."

Others around you, coax you to stay. "Come on. It's exciting!"

You start to think in that way and get okay with taking the ride. "Okay, you're right."

But you will flip flop between being afraid and being excited. And the thing is that you actually experience the same exact physical things with both emotions.

Only your brain sees one as positive – excitement. And it sees the other – fear – as negative. So, one is great as the other is unacceptable.

Chapter 6.7: Putting Reasoning Behind A Request

You've got a big favor to ask someone that you know won't want to do it.

What do you do?

You put a great reason why you need this done immediately behind your request.

"Can you clean out the gutters, honey?" You don't wait more than a beat to go on, "Because if it rains, and rain is in today's forecast, the water won't flow through the gutters and take it away from the house instead, it'll pool on the roof and we'll get leaks. We don't want that."

Most people will do things if they know there's a reason why it needs to be done.

Chapter 6.8: All Choices Lead To The Same Conclusion

In my opinion, this is the laziest of all the mind manipulation tricks. First of all, it shows no real insight into the human mind. Thinking that anyone, other than a very little kid, would truly believe that they only have three choices about anything is rather silly.

Let's say that you only have vanilla ice cream in the freezer and that's what you want your kid to pick. "So, you can have some apples for dessert. Or you can have some prunes. Or you can have vanilla ice cream."

What is any kid going to pick? *Ice cream.*

In the adult version of this, you might have a husband and wife who are house hunting. Tired of looking at every house on the market, the husband narrows it down to three houses. "You can pick the yellow one with the shady yard. You can pick the brown one with the big dining room. Or you can pick the blue one with the wrap around porch."

"Only those three? Why only them?" she'd ask. "There are fifty other ones to pick from. You're crazy if you think I'm going to just pick out of those."

The thing about all the house he gave her to pick from was that all of those had what he wanted in a home – a two-car garage. But she shot him down.

Maybe if he'd just been honest about wanting a two-car garage in the first place, his wife might've made that a priority to her as well.

Giving people the chance to work with you is a lot better than trying to trick them into getting them to do what you want.

Chapter 6.9: Assault On One's Identity

This is when someone attempts to tell you that you are not who you think you are. You are not a woman. You are not a wife. You are not someone's child. You are not anyone. You are not anything. You're void.

It might seem like something that no one would fall for, but if these mantras are repeated over and over again for extended periods of time, then most people do begin to believe that about themselves – *they are no one.*

Key Takeaways

- Using repetition will get you the results you are looking for.
- Imitating someone will make them feel more comfortable with you and more susceptible to your mental manipulations.
- Using don't in the place of can't make it seem like you have made the decision not to do something, instead of it not being allowed.
- Rituals help to cement things into your brain.
- Using excited instead of afraid can be a good way to trick your mind into experiencing negative things in a positive way.

- When you make a request, putting the reasoning behind that makes it more likely to be accepted.

- When offering choices when you are trying to manipulate them, you will want all the choices to come to the same conclusions.

- By assaulting someone's identity, you can break them down to nothing so that you can build them back up into the person you want them to be.

Exercises

You really want a house with a swimming pool, but you think your spouse won't want that. What technique would you use to get what you want and why?

If an officer of the law asks you to come down to the station to talk to them about a crime, what will you do about that?

If someone tells you that you are not who you think you are, how will you deal with that?

If you want someone to accept the things they must do, what would you implement to help them accept the fact?

Chapter 7: The Trojan In Your Head

Chapter 7.1: Introduction

We all have the ability to be our own worst enemies. People with bad intentions will use this against us if we allow them to.

Using mind games to mentally manipulate a person is an insidious act that tears at a person's sanity.

Anything that so deeply hurts and scars a person isn't nice to do and we all know that. Yet, we all have done some of these things and some of these things have been done to us.

Knowing what these things can do to a person will help you to know when you must use these mind tricks and when they are being used on you.

Once you can recognize these tricks as they are taking place, you won't become a victim of mind games anymore.

Chapter 7.2: Disqualifying

This act is really hurtful. You not only deliberately want to hurt someone's feelings, but you are also going to give them a double-shot of your viper tongue.

For example – Sheila doesn't like the fact that her friend, Ashley is prettier than her. So, she often uses a tactic to throw Ashely off about her appearance.

"You did not dye your hair again, Ashley? What a mistake," Sheila says very loudly, to purposely draw the attention of their classmates.

With wide eyes, Ashely runs her hand through her golden blonde hair. "What?"

Before everyone around them sees Sheila as a real meanie, she says, "I didn't mean to hurt your feelings, Ash – it's just that your hair looks like a haystack."

Double whammy!

Chapter 7.3: Forgetting

This age-old tactic for messing with someone's mind can be so mean that it defies reason.

Here's an example-

Jane came home from work with a splitting headache only to find that the aspirin bottle is empty. "Oh, Charlie took the last one and didn't bother to toss the empty bottle out so I would know that we had none left! I'll call him and ask him to please bring more home."

She did let her husband know about the aspirin then went to take a hot bath to see if that would help with the pain until he got home with the medicine.

But when he comes home with empty hands, she asks, "Where is the medicine, honey?"

"Oh, I forgot about that completely. I'm sorry."

"It was only a half-hour ago. How could you forget?"

"I got a call and drove past all the stores. Sorry."

He's not the one with a splitting headache and it's glaringly apparent that his wife doesn't rank very high on his caring meter.

Chapter 7.4: Persecuting

Have you ever been the one who does everything wrong?

Or have you been the one pointing out how someone else always does everything wrong?

Using persecution to make a person feel like less of a person is the way to go here. Telling them that they always let you down, lets them feel bad about themselves.

And if someone is telling you that you always do something that bothers them, then it's you who are at the wrong end of this deal.

Whichever end you are on, you can stop it from continuing. Simply state that no one is always or never anything. We all do things in varying degrees.

So, don't be this person and if you are the one being persecuted, then don't stand for it.

Chapter 7.5: Guilt Tripping

My mother lived to take us all on guilt trips. No matter how much easier it would've been to get us to do something, she had to go the extra mile to make us feel horrible over something first.

An actual guilt-tripping story here folks-

"Can you go out and bring in the Sunday paper?" she asked me.

I was a helpful kid. "Sure, Mom."

Just as I got to the paper that lay on the stone path in front of our home, the sprinkler came on and shot me right in the face. I grabbed the newspaper anyway and fled the scene. And just as I was shaking the water off my body, I saw my mother standing by the faucet. She'd turned it on, on purpose.

As if she hadn't noticed a thing, she held out her hand to receive the paper. I wasn't sure if she'd meant to soak me or not. Feeling confused, I walked up to her and just as before I got to her, I tripped over one of the stones that had been moved out of place.

I fell right into her, knowing her down on her bottom. "Why'd you do that?" she screamed at me.

"I tripped. I didn't do it on purpose." I scrambled up and reached out to take her hand to help her up.

"Don't touch me!" she snapped at me. "I can do it myself."

"Sorry," I said, and I meant it. I hadn't meant to knock her down at all.

"You got me all wet too. Yuck." She got up on her own with only a slightly damp spot on her shirt.

I was drenched. "Um." I gestured to my wet state.

Shaking her head as if she didn't even notice my current state, she snatched the paper from me then turned away from me. "Just give it to me. I asked a simple thing from you. I didn't realize it would cost me so much. Now my back hurts and my shirt is ruined. Thanks a lot."

Demoralized, I could only stand there, feeling guilty about what? I wasn't sure.

But there was lots of guilt and believe it or not, she got to keep me on that guilt trip for a solid week. I would be at her beck and call, doing everything she asked of me. And she asked a lot!

Chapter 7.6: Gaslighting

This mind trick is so dark that I hate even to let people know it exists. But I only do it so that you can see it when and if it happens to you.

Not everyone is handed this particular mind trick mostly because you have to be at least half-evil to play it.

So it goes like this – you know that what someone is saying really happened. But you want them to think they're losing their minds. And by the time you are finished with them, they just might.

Example –

"You know that coffee shop we used to go to all the time, Brad?" June asked her long-time boyfriend.

"You mean the ice cream shop, June. I don't even drink coffee," he said.

"No, it was a coffee shop. And you stopped drinking coffee a few years ago. But you and I did drink coffee when we first started dating." She recalls it perfectly.

"Not me, I guess," he states.

"It was you," she insists. "There was green trim around the tables. You remember. And that's where we found we loved caramel in our coffee."

Shaking his head, he's adamant. "I have never liked coffee, June. And I wouldn't even go into a coffee shop. It. Wasn't. Me."

"It was you!" She knows it was him. She doesn't recall ever going to that coffee shop with anyone else. And it's not the first time he's pulled this on her either.

If you find someone doing this to you, remove yourself from their company. They are the worst kind of manipulators who only seek to destroy everything about you.

Chapter 7.7: Shaming

People who shame others express themselves by trying to point out people who say or do something they want others to believe isn't morally right. It's when a person is so quick to point out things about others to everyone who will listen, so they don't look at them too hard.

I'm sure you've heard the expression when you're pointing at someone else, only one finger is aimed at them while you have three of your own fingers pointing back at you. This stems from people who love making others the center of ridicule, thusly taking the attention of others away from them.

As if they were even paying attention to them in the first place.

The worst part is that these people most often form jealousy about someone, then try to dig up anything on them to make them look bad. This is also known as piling up dead bodies to walk upon to make yourself look taller.

It's just bad mojo, karma, or whatever your particular idea of paying for the bad things you do is. I wouldn't use this at all, nor for any reason. If you truly have beef with someone, hash it out with them, without trying to defame them.

Chapter 7.8: Pretending

Why do people pretend about anything, you ask?

Well, to avoid dealing with honest emotions and conflict of course.

You could be out at a club and someone from the opposite sex might come up to you with some words that flatter you and you might actually believe that they're into you in a big way.

But here's the thing about situations like that and lots of others where people are able to make sexual advances without it seeming gross and unwanted. You have gone to a bar, a nightclub, a social situation of any kind really. This means you are out, and you might be looking for some action.

There are many people who simply want some sexual action and are willing to lie about their true interests just to get what they want. After the deed is done, they will disappear and refuse to take your calls and texts. They never wanted you for more than one thing.

Does this hurt?

Well, of course, it does. But the thing to know is that you shouldn't do an instant hookup anyway if you're vulnerable to being flattered and falling into bed with people who never meant a thing they said.

And never think that only the male gender of our human species does this, the females do this just as much as the males do.

What about when someone is mad, and they pretend not to be. Now, this one is done most often by females, but males can do it too. And the way this plays out is never nice either.

If a woman is mad and she says she's not, her man better walks on eggshells for the next week or even longer, and he better watch out for everything. She could merely wash his whites with reds to turn them pink, to cutting the brake lines on his car. It's that bad.

Chapter 7.9: Ghosting

Disappearing, not answering calls, or texts is sometimes seen as someone trying to avoid you or let you know that they're mad at you. And there are times that is true.

The main reason people ghost others is to see if others actually care about them.

Janice, "He's called eighteen times in the last three hours. Yeah, it's safe to say he does like me. But I'm still gonna leave him waiting the whole day to make sure he's into me."

If you find someone doing that to you, don't waste your time on them. They have a host of things you will have to go through before they ever admit their feelings for you if they're capable of forming real feelings in the first place.

The thing to know about people who do things like this, right from the very beginning, is they could have a personality disorder that might make living life with them in it extremely difficult.

Key Takeaways

- If someone tells you that they forgot something important you asked them to do, you should see this as a mind game.

- If you begin to feel as if someone is persecuting you, this is a mind game.

- Using guilt to get someone to do what you want them to is playing with a person's mind.

- Gaslighting is an insidious act that actually scrapes at a person's sanity, making them think that things happened that didn't or that things didn't happen then did.

- When someone tries to make you feel ashamed of something, they are using your mind against you.

- Pretending that you don't hear someone or see someone is just another mind game.
- Ghosting is used to get someone to miss you. Be above that.

Exercises

You're looking hot out at the club. But you're not looking for anything more than someone to dance with. So when Jane – the sexy babe asks you to dance, then starts telling you how she saw you across the room and couldn't take her eyes off you, do you jump right in and get on board with her taking you home?

A new man in your life has just told you that something you knew happened, didn't happen. What do you do next?

Your spouse has thrown out half your closet of clothes because they deemed them inappropriate and unflattering, what do you do?

Are playing mind games ever an okay thing to do to other people? And why or why not?

Chapter 8: Profiling A Victim

Chapter 8.1: Behaviors Of Those Most Susceptible To becoming Victims Of Dark Psychology

Mark, patsy, pawn, flunky, lackey, instrument, tool, softy, sucker, soft-touch, easy prey, easy target – all these words mean the same thing about a person – they are easy to fool. And it is people with these traits who become the victims of many mind tricks.

We've found out a lot about all the different mind tricks there are out there. And we've all done some of them and some of them have been done to us as well.

This list of words and informal definitions will let you know which of these characteristics you have. *Let's face it, we all have at least a few of them.*

And, if you bought this book so you could seek out victims, which I hope you did not, then you will find out what type of person will fall for your new-found wisdom. This will help you not to waste time on trying to mind-screw people who won't take it.

Also, people who are hard to trick, tend to be angry when they find someone using tactics they easily recognize, and most don't hesitate to call people out on it – alerting everyone they know of the predator in their midst. And that can be not only humiliating but cost you precious time in your dark endeavors.

The Disease to Please – This is one of my own weaknesses, so I can easily say that I've had to really work on this in my adult life. And I have been taken advantage of many times before I sought out information on the dark forces that surround us almost all the time.

At the pit of this problem is anxiety.

Not many understand that when they're killing themselves to put together lavish parties for the entire family – alone mind you. People pleasers don't ask for help and don't accept the help that is offered. *They can do it. They don't mind at all. You go have fun and leave the rest to them.*

Until I educated myself about this, I thought I was merely being a good person – not even a great one – just a good one.

I found out that I was really using mental manipulations to get people to like me – or pretend to. All that really mattered was that I wasn't disliked. And this led to other odd feelings inside of me.

Slaving away at whatever grandiose task I took on, I would end up extremely tired, broke from spending all my own money to do whatever I was doing, and eventually, I felt put out.

The kudos were great for a job well done, but they fell short of what I really needed for some reason. Then the resentments would begin. *I was such a fool! I'll never do that again.*

Yet I did, over and over again, until I found out that what I was doing was a vain attempt at escaping my underlying anxiety. The tasks I took on only enhanced the anxiety, making me work so much harder so that no one noticed how anxious I truly was.

Pleasing people makes you no friends. It makes you feel none the better about anything. It is a curtain that you pull around yourself, a sparkly one, to mask the mess behind it.

Only, it masks nothing and all who you've catered to see right through it. So, stop. You're an easy mark in many ways since you don't want to let anyone down.

Just say no. It is your right to do that. If anyone gets mad, upset, or whatever they get, so what?

Do you, because that's exactly what everyone else does. You can still take on big things, but let others help. If you don't let others help, you are denying them and actually making them dislike you.

In short, face your anxieties face-on and stop trying to hide them from yourself because many others see it anyway.

Addiction for Approval – "Is that okay with you?" isn't a thing you should have to ask unless we are talking about what a customer wants.

If you're making something for a person who is purchasing it, then you do want them to be satisfied with your product.

I'm talking about something like this –

Mary bought a dress she fell in love with earlier that day at a boutique she's been dying to try. So, she puts it on for a night out with her boyfriend. Running her hand along the fine stitching of the dress, she asks him, "Is this dress okay with you?"

Right there is where she messed up.

If she likes it and is okay with it, then that is all that matters. If he says he likes the dress of doesn't say a word, who cares?

She likes it.

When you need approval all the time – *Do you like the green beans this time, darling? I put bacon in them just for you.* You are setting yourself up for disappointment and making it well known that you are a patsy who is easily fooled.

You've all known of people who make a meal and put it on the table and leave the people with this message, "Eat it, don't eat it, but I made it and I expect no rude comments."

Be that person and let the part of you who needs approval slough off like dead skin off the heel of your foot. *Once it was a part of you and now it's not.*

Emotophobia – This is a fear of showing emotions. It can also mean the fear of having emotions although that's rare since most of us have emotions.

This comes from childhood trauma. You cried over normal things and were scolded for doing it.

More than once, I've attended funerals where the immediate family wasn't shedding even one tear. Sitting tall, stoic, and strong, they listened to the heartfelt service without seeming upset in the least. Meanwhile, in the test of the funeral home, people who weren't even as close as the immediate family sniffled, wept softly, and once I even heard a sob. None of the emotions going on with the rest of the people who'd gathered to pay their respects to the deceased rubbed off on the immediate family. They wanted to show how strong they truly were.

Not showing emotions that you feel isn't healthy – not mentally and not physically.

Emotions are just as much a part of us as our fingers and toes are. Would you ignore your fingers?

Would you eat like a dog, just to ignore your fingers?

No. No, you would not.

Don't try to ignore or hide your emotions. Not only because of the effects it has on your health but also because people who prey upon others see that as a weakness and put you into their line of sight to victimize you.

Inability to Assert One's Self or Say No – IMPORTANT!!! You can say no!!!

If someone asks you to do something, you can simply say, no.

If someone wants you to give them something, you can just say no.

You have to recall the phrase, 'Just say no,' from those drug commercials. If you can just say no to drugs, then you can just say no to cousin Joe who wants to borrow your car.

This goes hand in hand with people-pleasing. So that means that at its core, it is a thing people do to avoid anxiety. Telling people they won't do or give things can make the situation uneasy.

Okay, that is how it goes sometimes. Deal with it and move on so others don't see you as an easy target.

Soft Personal Boundaries – Do people stand too close in line behind you without you letting them know that it's bothering you?

Do people ask you to accept things that you aren't comfortable with?

Do you often find yourself feeling awkward?

If you said yes to any of these, you have soft personal boundaries.

You must get comfortable letting people know that you aren't okay with the things that you are not okay with. Honesty is key here.

Be honest with yourself first and others right after that. Again, if you allow anyone into your personal zone, you are taking risks that others won't.

Low on Self-Reliance – Do you know without a doubt that you are capable of taking care of yourself?

Do you feel that no matter what comes up, you can deal with it?

And that doesn't mean that you can go it alone either. It just means that if you find yourself alone, will you be able to do what it takes to feed yourself, have shelter, and do what it takes to stay alive.

Or do you feel that you could never make it on your own? Do you feel like you couldn't get a job and keep it? Do you feel like you can't pay all of your bills alone? Do you feel that you can't possibly live life alone – even for a little while?

If you feel this way, then you are making yourself into an easy target. Plus, you are putting yourself into such a vulnerable position that many villains will seek you out to use you.

Never feel like you can't do things on your own. If you have to seek government help, then do that. It's not as terrible as seeking help from people who are only looking to use you.

External Locus of Control – Most of us know that we have control of the things that happen to us. If we fail a test, then we accept that we didn't do enough research to pass it.

Others might blame them for failing on the teacher.

When you blame others for your own shortcomings, you are a person who isn't willing to look at themselves.

While that might not sound like you would be more vulnerable to becoming a victim, it does make you that way. You find reasons to blame others for all the mistakes you do – thus, you tend to make more mistakes than others who are striving and working hard not to make them in the first place.

Naiveté – What in the heck can you do about being naïve?

After all, life has to happen to you for you to understand what others are capable of.

So, there you have it. Let life happen to you. Don't keep yourself cooped up and away from other people. You have to get out there to understand life and how people are. That means getting hurt. That means getting lied to. That means getting bumps and bruises.

We can't get rid of the naiveté or innocence, unless we have relationships, try new things, and live our lives.

Not only do we rob ourselves of experiences, but we make ourselves open to being taken advantage of.

Over-conscientiousness – This might sound like it's not really a problem at all. After all, it's nice to think of others. But when you put what other people want so far ahead of what you want or think, then you can fall into the prey category.

Along with being over conscientiousness comes over agreeableness. If you tend to agree with people without finding out the facts for yourself, you can end up doing things you never thought you would do.

Being a disagreeable person might be something you don't want to be. But you have to be able to disagree with other people from time to time – not every time – but when you honestly don't agree with someone or something, then you must be true to yourself.

If you really think about this concept, you can look at why so many people followed Hitler. They not only agreed with his insane ideas, but his soldiers also carried out horrific mass murders for him as well.

Agree with only what you truly agree with. Be thoughtful of others, but not so thoughtful that you ignore your own wants and needs to hand all of what you need to someone else. Sharing is okay but giving all you have to anyone else is a mistake that you don't need to make.

This is one of the top five personality traits of prosocial behavior.

Over-intellectualization – Being smart is great. And who doesn't want to think like an intellectual at times?

Thinking intellectually when things come up all of a sudden and have to be dealt with without letting emotion get in your way – like a paramedic, doctor, fireman, etcetera – is what one must do to get the job done.

But what if the day to day problems come up and you still refuse to allow emotion to play a part in your decision making?

Your heart and feelings are part of the empathy system. If you can't have real feelings, then you can't understand how others truly feel. Most of us have been on the business end of the dental drill.

The reason why anxiety is such a huge part of going to the dentist is that our mouths are full of sensory receptors – part of why deep kisses feel so good that you don't want them to end. So, when you go to the dentist, you automatically know that your mouth is a sensitive area in the first place.

The shrill sound of the drill already alerts the primary senses that make your brain say, "Get away from that sound – it means bad things for you!"

And when a dentist doesn't allow enough time for the numbing agent to work, that means and things for you. Who hasn't been in that scenario?

That's why we hate going to the dentist. Way too many times, you've been told that it's not really pain, just pressure. That's to make the process go faster and the next patient can be seen.

But here's the thing that really makes this crazy. They are absolutely right. It is just pressure that you feel while your mouth is numbed – even a little. You're more afraid of the noise that the drill is making than of any real pain.

Plus, the dust-like particles flying out of your mouth can make your brain think that way more harm than good is occurring inside your mouth. And you use that thing to kiss with, so you don't want damage done to it.

In my opinion, the dentistry industry could make this thing quitter – the same way you can put a silencer on a firearm, you could most likely do the same thing with a dental drill.

If you take a look at this rather simple procedure, you will find that most of us over-intellectualize it. Your mouth. The drill. Pain instead of pressure. And ultimately – messing with your kisser. When it's all just really pressure.

Emotional Dependency – You've heard about being dependent on someone of course. Financial independence is something that we are born into. Emotional dependency is another beast altogether.

When a person has a need for another person that is overwhelming – they can't live without them – then they may have what is clinically termed, dependent personality disorder.

This disorder can lead the person to become submissive to the point that they will not get their own needs met at all. And the fear of being separated from the person they're dependent on is so great, they live with basically perpetual anxiety. Can you imagine needing someone so much that you didn't think you could live without them? Can you imagine not knowing how you could find a way to make a living, take care of putting a roof over your own head, and finding a way to but food to eat?

Scary stuff.

Most of the time, this particular disorder doesn't begin when you're a kid. Rather it manifests in the early years of adulthood.

Now, most of us are a bit wary of having to provide for ourselves and even live alone. For that reason, many young adults tend to find roommates or friends who they can get together and rent a home or apartment with, sharing the bills and chores to make life a bit easier.

It's during this phase of life that people with the disorder begin to sink, instead of swimming. They begin looking for someone to take care of them without even realizing what they're doing.

It's an innate action that comes in response to the growing fear that they can't make it on their own. Once the roommates begin to leave the nest, going on to join other relationships as most people do, the need becomes more apparent and at times the person can seem completely desperate to find someone to take care of them.

And in return for this enormous favor, they will – quite literally – do anything for the person willing to take care of them and never leave them. And I do mean anything.

They will allow things to happen to them that others wouldn't. The thing that comes along with someone being so needy, is that their demeanor can turn a person with a controlling personality – because, let's face it, only a person who seeks control over another human being is going to take on this person – into a real monster.

If they know that they can not only control every action of their victim, then they will go on to push their limits to see just how far they can go before the person finds a backbone to stand up to them. But these people don't have any limits. They will take whatever is dished out to them because they are terrified of being alone and supporting themselves, both financially and mentally.

You might think that the people with this disorder could seek out a companion who isn't controlling.

Well, you would be wrong. Most people want to help their loved ones achieve success, both mentally and financially. Normal people want to make sure the person they love knows how to care for themselves in all ways. After all, we all die. There is a one hundred percent chance that you will lose the people you love to death or you will die before they do, leaving them to deal with the loss.

What this means is that the dependent personality will shy away from those who want to help them find their footing. They want someone to carry them, not try to force them to find a way to become emotionally equipped to stand on their own two feet.

About the only way you can truly help an individual with this disorder is to encourage them to seek psychological help to learn how to deal with this tremendous anxiety that will eventually lead them into a life of submissiveness and abuse at the hands of the person they put their lives into.

Dependent – Of course, there are varying degrees of dependency. Some only need financial dependence to get them through their lives. They have the emotional thing down, it's just the money factor that freaks them out.

We all know a few people who seem to refuse to work. They have many reasons why they don't want to or can't work. So, they must find someone who is willing to do all the work, pay all the bills, and they must do this to the satisfaction of the financially dependent person.

In this case, the roles are reversed from being emotionally dependent. The dependent person plays the dominating role here, instead of the submissive role.

This might sound insane, but it's true. They find a person who has worked most of their lives and has the mentality that work is a thing they must do, no matter what. Most of the time, the person they seek already has established bank accounts, a home, automobiles, and credit. Great credit is the key to this whole thing.

That's because the dependent person needs to know for certain that their intended victim has everything they will need in their lives. They like to live well, and that won't happen if they don't pick someone who is not only a great worker but also financially savvy.

Like most things, the dependent person doesn't act like they're this way at all. Most of them get a job at a place where they can meet someone who actually likes to work. They'll act as if they have had some rough patches in their past that's left them with an old junky car – if they have one at all – and having to live with their parents, along with either never building credit in the first place or having a past relationship that had the other person ruining what had been stellar credit.

So, along with being a great worker with financial sense, their intended victim must also have a great sense of sympathy and empathy. Making their intended feel sorry for them is step one in the process of getting what they want.

Once they're in the heart of their victim, and in their home, this is when something tragic will happen that has them getting fired or having to quit their job. Either a strange illness, such as stomach troubles or back pain that they claim to have seen a doctor for and there seems to be nothing that can be done but allows time to fix what ails them.

Just after leaving their job, they will have a miraculous recovery – *oh, glory to the highest* – and now the reason they can't work will change from illness to no one will hire me. They will pretend to be job seeking while really out doing whatever they want while spending the money their loved one gave them to help them with their job search – while driving the car they gave them to get to a new job once they get one.

This becomes a hamster wheel as the provider will allow this to go on for only so long – granted this could go on for years – before the provider gets sick and tired of how their dependent spends all of their hard-earned money. Their credit becomes less than stellar because their dependent continuously holds out a carrot in front of their noses, promising that with this new purchase, they're sure to get a job to pay the payment. But then no job comes around, the payment can't be made and there goes the provider's credit in no time at all.

And the really sad part of this is that once they've sucked their provider dry, they use the excuse that their provider has become a loser who they can't abide anymore and they will end that relationship to find another victim they can suck dry.

Vampire syndrome would be a great term for this personality disorder.

So, beware of the vampire who will have their charms and their insatiable thirst, not for your blood, but for your money.

Immature – Dealing with an immature person is not only annoying, but it's also something that can make a person stark raving mad. And the thing about this disorder is that it can't be hidden.

When someone gets involved with an immature person, they're well aware of what they're getting into. Or so they think anyway.

Most people who get involved with a person with this disorder probably think that the person will grow up one day. And they're lots of fun to be with since they're so spirited and outgoing.

But the bad thing about being with an immature person is that everything is a big joke to them. And I mean everything.

If you end up with an immature person, you might be sitting in your recliner, watching some television when all of a sudden your drenched because they brought in the garden hose and let loose on you, laughing like a hyena the whole time. And they never clean up their messes either.

You're left wet and having to clean up a wet mess —
all the while having to listen as they laugh and say
how you should've seen your face!

Impressionable — Most children are
impressionable, and this is exactly why you keep
them away from people who curse or exhibit other
bad behavior. Your kid will end up acting like them
if they're allowed to be around them too much,
rubbing off on them.

In the case of being an impressionable adult, this
becomes a problem that's much bigger than using
bad language. This can mean that you will be much
more susceptible to being scammed or used to do
someone else's dirty work.

And your opinions can be swayed quite easily as
well. As if you have no mind of your own, you will
go back and forth, agreeing with things you have
just agreed with on the opposite end of the
spectrum.

Trusting – You can't trust everyone to tell you the truth. You can't trust everyone to do what they say they will. And you can't trust everyone with the things you hold dear – your family, your money, your belongings.

You've heard the horror stories of people who hired a babysitter, fully trusting her with their children on to find out that they did unspeakable things to them in their absence.

So, what do you do when someone says all the right things, and acts all the right ways but is a complete liar and a savage to boot?

This is why surveillance systems came to be. And you should let people know that they are being videoed as well. This will keep them honest and on their toes. People don't want to get caught in their bad acts, so they don't often do them right in front of a camera.

But the best thing to do is to really know a person and their background, know other people that have known them a long time too before you go giving them access to anything you hold dear or giving them important responsibilities to deal with.

Carelessness – This is one of those lazy things some people do. At times, most of us have careless moments. But most of us try not to have them because they lead to more work than we had in the first place.

When someone is continuously careless, it causes more work for everyone else and things get broken or destroyed due to their careless behavior. Needless to say, not many people care to have perpetually careless people around them or their things.

Lonely – Loneliness can have you making bad decisions. If you just want someone – anyone – around, then you will find mostly the villains in this world seeking to entertain you.

Find a friend in yourself. It's actually very nice to visit a library alone and let the characters of some book fill that void until you find yourself feeling whole again.

When you're whole, you attract the right kind of people. When you're down, weak, lonely – you attract predators – just like in the wild, nature will take its course.

Narcissistic – This word has become a thing we hear all the time now for some reason. Is it because so many people have had this personality disorder and it's just now been given a name?

No. It's the invention of social media that has alerted us that so many people have this disorder.

So, what is narcissism – besides being hard to spell?

Wikipedia defines it as such - **Narcissism** is the pursuit of gratification from vanity or egotistic admiration of one's idealized self-image and attributes. This includes self-flattery, perfectionism, and arrogance. The term originated from Greek mythology, where the young Narcissus fell in love with his own image reflected in a pool of water.

So, there you have it in a nutshell.

Altruistic – Exactly the opposite of narcissism, being altruistic means that you will self-sacrifice, self-deny, and be completely unselfish and you will cater to others.

Also, not a healthy way to be. A lot of mothers fall into this disorder without knowing they ever were falling in the first place. It's second nature to give up things for your baby. When you're pregnant, you give up alcohol and anything else that might hurt that baby. When it's born, you give up sleep, give up time, give up on getting that two-hour bath you used to take.

So, little by little, you end up giving and giving and self-denying until you wake up one day and realize what you've done.

Not to worry, everyone will still love you when you take time to do you. After all, they are your family and you've instilled a ton of love into them.

Impulsive – Being impulsive might sound fun and whimsical but when you're an adult, making big decisions, impulsiveness isn't a good thing.

Save that for picking up some flowers on the way home for your girl and leave the snap decisions right there.

Frugal – Being a bit frugal is great. Being totally frugal – where you refuse to pay full price for anything – is not.

Why? You ask.

When you are willing to take knock-offs in place of name brands, sometimes that's a good idea. But a quality product is worth the money. And when you're a real bargain hunter, people will see that – because people like this can't stay quiet about how they won't pay full price for things – so that means they can scam these people with relative ease.

Learning how to be quiet about your thrifty nature is step one. Step two is understanding that you can pay a thousand dollars for a refrigerator that will last for fifteen years. Or you can pay a hundred bucks on a used fridge that will last you maybe a year, tops. You save money in the long run if you go ahead and pay top dollar for the things that matter.

Materialistic – Opposite of frugal, people who are materialistic spend copious amounts of money on things that don't matter. And the more they spend on an item, the louder they boost about it.

Paying a thousand dollars for a pair of shoes is plain stupid. I don't care if they will last your entire life, it's still a materialistic purchase meant to try to make people envious of you.

Masochistic – If you like pain or tedious activities, you are – by definition – a masochist. But what does this mean about making you an easy target?

Believe it or not, there is a vulnerability about you that you don't know about. You're so set on pushing your limits that you will get involved in the most heinous of activities that put you in positions that will leave you even more vulnerable.

Imagine that you are tied up, at the mercy of a total stranger at your own home when they suddenly stop pleasuring you with pain so they can rob you blind.

Oh, but you like pain, so you might not be put off by the pain of having to buy all new things.

Greedy – You would think that greedy people are the villains at all times. But the thing about being greedy means you're a pretty easy mark when it comes to scams.

Look at this situation. You're a greedy person in a grocery store. The less than reputable store has salesmen planted in the produce area to try to get the older produce sold.

So, the incognito salesman points out that the tomatoes are about to go up, according to a news report he just saw. It's rumored that everyone is going to storm their local markets to get all the tomatoes that they can.

When the greedy person hears this, he quickly begins to get way more than his fair share of the nearing the rotten stage veggies.

See how greed can work against you?

The Elderly - We all come from our own generations and by the time we get old, so many new things are going on that we lose track of them all. And our brains aren't as young as they used to be – neurons fire at a much lower rate in the majority of the elderly folks.

We've all heard of scam after scam done over the phone to people of higher ages. They hear that a grandson is locked in a Mexican prison and he only needs a thousand bucks to get out of jail. All they have to do is send them money and they will gladly get her loved one out.

Poor Grandma barely makes it on what she gets from her social security, but she's got to save her grandson with the small amount of savings she has left from her and her late husband's savings account.

This is why it's important to watch out for your elderly relatives and friends.

Key Takeaways

- Knowing about yourself and your shortcomings shouldn't be a thing you feel shamed about or embarrassed of. We all have at least one of these things and knowing that about ourselves will save us lots in the long run.

Exercises

If you will only pay less than half price on things, does this make you smart or vulnerable?

If you like to flaunt your expensive purchases what type of person are you?

Looking at yourself all the time, thinking about what you want and what makes you happy takes up most of your time, makes you have what sort of tendencies?

When people test their pain limits what is this called?

Is it always okay to buy cheaper products instead of products with a proven track record that is worth the money asked for them?

Conclusion

The information that you have just read isn't meant to hurt your feelings. It's not meant to make you feel bad about yourself. This information is only to help you in your life.

Knowing our weaknesses and faults only enhance our lives. Knowing things about yourself will only help you.

And if you have read this book purely to learn how to make others do what you want them to, then you should think about karma and what's right and wrong for a bit.

Last but not least, never forget that all of us are exposed to a constant stream of manipulation in our ever day lives – whether it's through the ads on the internet or TV, by a local politician trying to win the next election or your spouse trying to convince you to what that movie together.

What makes manipulation so hard to recognize and block is not its finesse or complexity. Rather the opposite is the case. Manipulation is often so trivial and omnipresent that we simply fail to see the wood for the trees.

The end.

Thank you again for purchasing this book!

If you liked the book, please add a review on Amazon!

Reviews are crucial for a book to thrive on Amazon; otherwise it will simply die away.

Hence our survival as authors and publishers heavily depends on them.

So, if you found this book useful in any way, I would be delighted to see a review from you with a simple feedback on what you liked and what can be improved.

Thank you so much!

Sources And References

Wikipedia (2019) Dark Triad retrieved from
https://en.wikipedia.org/wiki/Dark_triad

McLeod, S. A. (2019). What is psychology?. Retrieved from
https://www.simplypsychology.org/whatispsychology.html

Goulston M.D., F.A.P.A., Mark (2013) Never be Manipulated
Again Retrieved from
https://www.psychologytoday.com/us/blog/just-listen/201312/never-be-manipulated-again

Psychology Today (2019) Deception retrieved from
https://www.psychologytoday.com/us/basics/deception

Cherry, Kendra (2019) Psychology of Persuasion and Social
Influence Retrieved from
https://www.verywellmind.com/what-is-persuasion-2795892

Wikipedia (2019) Covert Hypnosis retrieved from
https://en.wikipedia.org/wiki/Covert_hypnosis

Parvez, Hanan (2015) Covert Hypnosis Techniques for Mind
Control Retrieved from
https://www.psychmechanics.com/conversational-or-covert-hypnosis/

Hutton, George (2014) Mind Persuasion Retrieved from https://mindpersuasion.com/covert-hypnosis-techniques-for-easy-influence/

Dachis, Adam (2012) Brainwashing Techniques You Encounter Everyday (and How to Avoid Them) Retrieved from https://lifehacker.com/brainwashing-techniques-you-encounter-every-day-and-ho-5886571

Layton, Julia (2019) How Brainwashing Works Retrieved from https://science.howstuffworks.com/life/inside-the-mind/human-brain/brainwashing1.htm

Pickett, Paul K – Pickett, Lesia (2014) 6 Creepy Brainwashing Techniques You Can Use Today Retrieved from https://www.cracked.com/article_21309_6-incredible-ways-you-can-use-words-to-brainwash-people.html

Loewen, Stanley (2012) How to Handle People Who Play Mind Games With You Retrieved from https://www.healthguidance.org/entry/16146/1/how-to-handle-people-who-play-mind-games-with-you.html

Schoenewolf, Ph.D, Gerald (2016) Mind Games People Play Retrieved from https://blogs.psychcentral.com/psychoanalysis-now/2016/01/mind-games-people-play/